Whole Mind
HEALING

A Simple Path for Changing Your Life
by Healing Your Mind

Michael R. Kandle, Psy.D.

Whole Mind Healing
A Simple Path for Changing Your Life by Healing Your Mind

ISBN: 978-0-578-45249-4

Dedication

For my beloved wife Louise and dear son William, whose endless supply of love sustains my own endless healing.

Acknowledgements

Writing <u>Whole Mine Healing</u> was a labor *of, with* and *for* love. It was only possible because of my love of the subject, supported with the love I received from family and friends, and because healing is for the sake of love.

For their generosity of time, knowledge, advice, editing and encouragement, I am forever indebted to Benjamin Garber, Ph.D., Jeffrey Kinghorn, Laura Prescott, M.A., and Robert Haskins, Ph.D. Each believed in me and in the value of this work. Without them I could not have delivered this baby.

Special recognition is owed to Lucia Capacchione, Ph.D., the progenitor of the two-handed writing technique. Reading her seminal book, <u>The Power of Your Other Hand</u> (1988, 2019) began a revolution in my own healing experience and transformed my clinical work. More than 25 years later, Lucia responded to my outreach for consultation on <u>Whole Mind Healing</u>, offering indispensable guidance drawn from years as a talented healer and author herself.

To my wife Louise, son William, sister Ann, and dear friends Lori, Katie and Foad - thank you from the bottom of my heart for your abundant supply of love and encouragement.

Contents

Introduction

<u>Whole Mind Healing</u> is a book that will teach you how to heal your whole mind. You'll be surprised to discover how much easier this is to do than you might think, and how it's entirely possible to do by yourself. To do so, you'll need to learn about the process of healing and develop an understanding of the nature of your mind. What most people don't understand about their mind is that it's not a single entity, but rather is made up of multiple *subpersonalities*. By understanding the nature of these subpersonalities, a person can heal their whole mind.

The word *whole* in the title of this book has two integral meanings. The first refers to the *entirety* of all the mind's individual parts, and the second refers to the *wholeness* of the mind, a condition reflecting how well the individual parts are integrated through their relationships with one another. In many ways a mind is identical in nature to that of a family. Both are made up of three dimensions: the *individuals* (parts), the *whole* (collective), and the *relationships* between their parts. Together, the status of these dimensions determine how healthy a family or a mind will be. In a mind or a family, healthy functioning is determined by the health of each individual part and the health of the relationships between them. Because of this, healing is often required on both individual and relationship dimensions.

Why might a mind need to be healed in the first place? Most often this is because various painful or traumatic experiences have created scars, divisions, and conflicts within it. Returning to the family analogy, if an emotionally unhealthy parent abuses a child, this typically causes damage to that child as well as damage to the parent/child and spousal relationships in the family. For such a family to become whole and healthy again, individual healing would likely be necessary for the child, the unhealthy parent, and all the family relationships harmed by the abuse. A mind becomes wounded, and whole again, in the same way.

Most people don't think of their minds as consisting of separate and unique parts, nor that there can be multiple conflicts between them. Once you learn about the different subpersonalities in your mind and how to access them, you'll come to understand their different natures, their conflicts, and learn how they need to be healed.

Conflicts between subpersonalities result in a loss of internal connections – connections necessary for the mind to be whole rather than divided. The more the mind is divided, the more one's health becomes afflicted by anxiety, depression, anger, guilt, shame, and/or despair. Conflicted minds are also associated with parallel conflicts in relationships with others. This is because there is a direct correlation between how different subpersonalities relate internally and how they relate to the corresponding subpersonalities in others. Healing inner conflicts also helps manage outer conflicts. In other words, by learning to heal your mind you will also learn how to create healthier relationships with others.

The secret to both inner and outer healing can actually be discovered in a deeper understanding of the "Golden Rule." The Golden Rule is the most universal principle found in virtually every major religion and society, both around the world and across the span of history. The language of the Golden Rule varies slightly between different religious and secular traditions, but the fundamental wisdom is the same—that we must understand and treat others the way we would like others to understand and treat us. Though this may sound simple on the surface, there is more wisdom in this tenet than most people realize. This is *not* a book about religious principles or spiritual healing, but instead about the *process* of healing with the love and compassion represented in the Golden Rule.

There is nothing magical or mysterious about the healing process. Virtually everyone can learn how to do it. Though healing most often occurs in a therapeutic or other compassionate relationship, it can also be done by oneself. Either way, the healing process is a *relational* one.

This means that healing occurs through the interactions of a compassionate relationship. With respect to healing the mind, it's the relationships between subpersonalities where healing takes place. This is accomplished by replacing toxic beliefs and conflicted interactions with better understandings and collaborative partnerships. Whole Mind Healing will teach you exactly how this can be done.

In the chapters that follow, you'll be introduced to some concepts that may or may not be familiar to you. These include a map of the mind's different domains, the process for healing the relationships between them, and a simple, effective technique for *applying* the healing process wherever wounds require healing. Though these concepts may be unfamiliar, there is very little contained in Whole Mind Healing that is new or unconventional. Everything presented here has roots in the traditions of mainstream psychology, philosophy, and ancient wisdom. The first part of Whole Mind Healing introduces the principles of the healing process, the second part provides a map of the mind, and the third part focuses on the experience of applying the principles of healing to the mind. It's written in a way that teaches readers how to heal their minds independently, though these lessons can also be adopted into an existing therapeutic relationship. The more choices we have in life the better. There is no "one size fits all" path to healing.

Throughout <u>Whole Mind Healing</u>, the terms *healing, creating peace,* and *conflict management* are used interchangeably because these functions rely on the same process, though with slightly different aims. Not all internal or external relationships can fully heal, yet there is still the potential for increasing peace and/or reducing conflicts within yourself and with others. <u>Whole Mind Healing</u> also places emphasis on the importance of personal safety. If deep and delicate sensitivities are encountered, guidance will be offered for how to maintain emotional safety and draw on outside support when necessary. Healing is most necessary in those places where people are most vulnerable, so healing must take place in safe conditions. I hope you will find this path easy to understand and to experience. If so, <u>Whole Mind Healing</u> will have fulfilled its purpose.

PART I

The Principles of Healing

CHAPTER 1

Healing: The Art of Managing Conflict

Conflict is everywhere in our lives, though hopefully not at all times. Conflict exists between ourselves and our loved ones – our families, spouses, parents, children, and friends. It also exists between ourselves and our workplace associates, other drivers on the road, authority figures in the world, and people we encounter who are just different from us in one way or another. The potential for conflict is constant, spanning the range from minor disagreements to all-out war. Wherever there are *others* there will eventually be some form of conflict with them. Some people choose to isolate themselves in order to minimize the harms of conflict, simply escaping conflicts with the world by avoiding others as much as humanly possible. One modern-day version of this isolation is to dwell in the virtual reality of the electronic world. In so many ways it's safer to observe and interact with the world through the relative safety of a computer, smartphone, or other electronic device that shields us from the vulnerabilities of face-to-face interaction. However, if we want to experience healing in the context of face-to-face relationships, we must learn the skills for managing conflict.

Others are most likely to disturb your peace when their values are in contrast to your own. Contrasting values create conflict, often generating fear, anger, and competition to resolve those conflicts. The subconscious mind reacts instinctively in ways that are oppositional in nature, further perpetuating conflict. This is true even in relationships with people whom we know and love. The most primitive part of the human mind reacts to conflicting values by judging them as "wrong", "bad", or "evil", and then prepares to hate, reject, avoid, fight, or possibly destroy them. These are the black-and-white reactions we have when we feel most threatened by others who are different from us. But, just because these reactions may be our most instinctive, it doesn't mean they are the *best* reactions to have when encountering others whose interests conflict with our own. There are better ways of reacting to others with whom we have conflict, ways that can transform the threat of opposition into potential opportunities for more peaceful relationships. This is what the art of conflict management is all about.

Learning the art of conflict management does not mean that you eliminate conflict from your life. Peace and conflict need to be thought of as belonging on different ends of a shared continuum rather than existing separately. We exist neither in a state of complete peace without conflict, nor in complete conflict without peace. They are relative to one another, and all relationships involve a blend of peace and conflict. The aim is to learn skills for living as much as possible on the peaceful side of this continuum. Doing so will not mean eliminating conflict from your life, but rather learning to move relationships further from the conflict end of the continuum toward the peaceful end by using the most effective skills for doing so.

If you were to consider pursuing peace by way of isolation, peace might still prove elusive. This is because conflict does not just occur with others in your outer world, but also occurs within you. How can that be? If you were the only person stranded on a remote island, how could your peace possibly be disturbed by conflict? As will be explained in part 2, the answer has to do with the fact that within each of us there resides a collection of different parts of our nature that represent very different sets of needs and values, and these parts naturally conflict with one another just as naturally as separate people conflict with one another.

Fortunately, the skills for managing conflict with other people are the same as those for managing conflicts, increasing peace, and healing within your own mind. A key premise of this book is that as you learn how to heal your own mind you will also be learning how to heal damaged relationships and maintain peace with others. Because of these parallel dynamics between inner and outer relationships, it's also possible to discover unknown internal conflicts by examining the types of conflicts you have with others.

The fundamentals of healing, both with others and within oneself, are fairly simple to understand. Put simply, *healing is a matter of repairing conflict by transforming division into wholeness, and conflict into collaboration.* Opposition is the most instinctive response to conflict, though in reality there are actually two ways to respond to any conflict. When oppositional reactions occur, conflict is resolved through a *contest* of wills; whoever exerts greater willpower prevails in the "resolution" of that conflict. The second option for responding to conflict is through a *collaboration* of wills. Under these circumstances, the conflicting partners find ways of working together to either resolve or manage the conflict.

The differences between oppositional and collaborative responses to conflict are significant. Oppositional behaviors are much more threatening than collaborative behaviors. They tend to be more judgmental, antagonistic, hostile, divisive, and sometimes harmful. Conflicts settled through opposition result in there being a winner and a loser (or possibly two losers in a draw), and there can be damage to the relationship between the conflicting parties. In contrast, conflicts managed collaboratively are less threatening, judgmental, hostile, divisive, and harmful. In the end, collaboration tends to yield two winners and allows for the relationship between the conflicting parties to remain intact or possibly even improve. By contrast, opposition is more likely to produce enemies and divisions. Collaboration tends to strengthen partnerships and result in goodwill and integration. Perhaps the greatest difference between opposition and collaboration is that the former is harmful to wholeness and the latter promotes wholeness. Therefore, everything following in this book will be about the process of managing conflicts by learning how to transform opposition into collaboration.

CHAPTER 2

Reprogramming Your Mind
for Healing and Peace

Like computers, the subconscious mind is loaded with programs. Some
of these programs were written and inherited prior to birth, such as
survival instincts that are written into our genetic codes. After birth
the subconscious acquires many other programs from parents, other
family members, school teachers, religious leaders, peers, and a wide
range of social norms. Together, these programs in the subconscious
become analogous to the operating system (OS) on a computer. All
new computers come with operating systems already installed, and then
we add other programs onto our computer to suit our various needs.
But the OS on a computer is the master program that organizes and
determines how well all other subsequent programs will function on
that computer. When there are "bugs" in the OS, these will interfere
with your computer's efficiency in running all of your other programs
and managing your data. Therefore, OS's are constantly being upgraded

and computer owners receive frequent reminders to install these OS upgrades to improve the performance of their computers.

The subconscious mind has programs that operate at different levels of awareness, and the most important programs (analogous to a computer's OS) function at the most subconscious level of the mind. Because these fundamental codes lie beneath our conscious awareness, they function automatically and seldom change. But that is not to say they are inaccessible or impossible to modify (or upgrade). The deepest programs in the mind are concerned with our needs for survival and are therefore quite primitive. One of these programs is designed to help us cope when we face life threatening dangers and conflicts. We are all familiar with the fight or flight instinct that is automatically activated whenever we perceive some form of threat or challenge. This instinct gets activated to some degree in every conflict situation that threatens our security and peace. By nature, the fight or flight instinct is an oppositional one that perceives the threatening party as some form of opponent that either needs to be fought or escaped. This instinct, while enormously important for our survival, can also be the greatest impediment to our peace of mind.

If your goal is to increase the amount of peace in your life, your mind's OS for dealing with conflict is going to require some upgrades. The programs for managing conflict collaboratively are not nearly as old, familiar, or pre-installed in our psyches as the more primitive oppositional programs are. In order for this reprogramming of the mind for healing and peace to be successful, some new programs will first need to be learned, and then installed into the subconscious mind where they can operate automatically. This will not put them on an equivalent plane with your primitive and pre-installed survival programs, but they will be able to eventually function as part of your "second nature."

A second analogy that might be helpful for understanding this process is to consider the function of a country's constitution. A constitution defines a country's core values and the system that will be used to govern it. Many other laws will be drawn up after a constitution is established, but all such laws must conform to the foundational principles of the constitution itself. A constitution is a highly durable code that cannot be changed often or easily. The U.S. constitution has only been amended 27 times in 250 years, and for very good reasons. It embodies the rules that our country depends on for its long term survival and therefore it must be protected from the whims of changing political and social moods. Just as changing a country's constitution requires very careful deliberation before new amendments to it are adopted, it's similarly important that any new program for the human mind be carefully weighed prior to adopting it into the governing system of the subconscious mind.

Many people believe that the programs imprinted on them by their creators (i.e., God, ancestral genes, parental values) should never be questioned, challenged or altered. But what if there are problems with these programs that limit or disturb your peace? And what if there are better programs that can promote greater peace and wholeness for your mind? These are choices you are free to make for yourself rather than to have them indelibly installed by others. Be assured that your subconscious programs will not in any way be altered just by reading this book. Only if the principles for healing and peace explained here are determined to be safe and desirable should you choose to install them into your own mind. Doing so will require some active effort and time; this process will be explained in part 4 of the book.

CHAPTER 3

The Five Pillars of Healing

Reprogramming the mind for healing requires making adjustments in your beliefs, intentions, thinking, feelings, and behavior. I refer to these as the five pillars of healing. Not only do these five pillars need to be adjusted, it's also necessary for them to be integrated with one another. How these five pillars function together will constitute a new program for healing and peace in your mind and in your life.

Let's change metaphors now. Imagine that your mind is like an enormous forest with hundreds of well-travelled paths to take toward different destinations under different circumstances. These paths have been a part of the forest of your mind since your earliest years. They are so well known to you that they can be navigated with little or no conscious effort. In this metaphor, the paths represent a network for your beliefs, intentions, thoughts, feelings, and behaviors. That represents a lot of information to process which would be overwhelming if you needed to figure it all out at once. Fortunately, your subconscious mind automatically knows which paths to take under many different circumstances. However, when it comes to conflict situations, these automatic paths will not always serve you well. You may have a program that favors some form of fight response or one that favors flight instead. Either of these may be best under some circumstances, but not most. In too many other circumstances, taking these paths will make things worse for you. In other words, just because these responses are easy and automatic does not mean that they are optimal for meeting your needs.

Now imagine that you can carve out new paths in the forest that may lead to much better outcomes when you are faced with conflict. Imagine that you are offered a set of blueprints for creating these new paths of belief, intention, thinking, feeling, and behavior. Such a map may be worth considering. It's entirely possible to create new paths in the forest of your mind in ways that can change your life. Chapters 4-8 will describe the five pillars of healing and peace that make up these new pathways and explain their significance for the creation and maintenance of peaceful wholeness in your life.

CHAPTER 4

Belief

Ontology is the branch of metaphysics that addresses the nature of existence. An essentially ontological question pertains to how things exist in the world. For instance, are all things existing in the world made up of a common element (a belief known as monism), or are there essential differences between elements in ways that make them fundamentally separate (a belief known as dualism)? Common examples of dualistic beliefs would be that mind and matter, good and evil, the natural world and the spiritual world are all fundamentally different and separate from one another. The idea that all things in existence are actually variations of a common element is most commonly associated with Albert Einstein's theory of relativity, in which he revealed that matter and energy are two versions of the same thing ($E=mc^2$). Likewise, quantum physics has demonstrated that particles and waves are two versions of a common reality which differ only when observed from different perspectives.

The reason for considering these contrasting theories of reality is because they have profound influences over the way we understand our relationships with others, as well as how we understand ourselves. Where dualism might suggest that heads and tails are two separate realities, monism would suggest that they are simply two contrasting sides of a singular coin. If you think about others as being fundamentally different from yourself, this limits the potential for recognizing your shared identity with them. However, if you believe that others are actually another version of who you are, then you can learn to recognize a shared identity with them.

The impact of your belief system is most clear when you consider the notions of good and evil. If what you believe to be good and evil are thought to be entirely separate elements of reality, then you will believe that the conflicts between them can only be dealt with in an oppositional way. This is a form of black-and-white thinking that generates fear, judgment, hatred, aggression, and war. Compare this to the monistic perspective on good and evil, which suggests that both coexist as parts of human nature, and that every individual has the capacity for good and evil within themselves. Demonizing, hating, and battling evil would then be a matter of demonizing, hating, and battling parts of yourself. Everyone has parts of themselves that they dislike intensely when these parts are perceived as sources of great trouble and distress. The two pioneers of psychoanalysis recognized this over a century ago. Sigmund Freud referred to such parts as belonging to the "id" of the psyche, and Carl Jung discussed how they belonged to the "shadow" level of the mind. Ever since, psychologists have studied how the conflicts people have with the dark sides of their own nature have resulted in all forms of psychological suffering. Fortunately, much has been learned about healthier ways to understand and regulate the conflicting parts of the human mind.

For the purposes of enjoying a healthier mind and more healthy relationships, there is great value in a belief system that recognizes the oneness of all beings. There are numerous references to this notion in the Bible and virtually every religion throughout the world. This is the notion that we must regard and treat others as we do ourselves, and this Golden Rule is the principle that is the most universal principle for peace and wholeness accepted by all religions throughout history. More will be said about this in chapter 6.

CHAPTER 5

Intention

Your intentions are like compass headings that keep your mind on course toward your goals. Establishing your intention is a simple yet influential step in preparing for any destination in life, including healing and peace. The forest of your mind is full of potential paths leading to different outcomes, and every fork represents a choice between contrasting values. Rather than choosing paths out of habit, setting clear intentions can help you choose more effective paths that you might not otherwise think about. This is why paying attention to your intentions is so meaningful. So many of your thoughts, feelings, and actions occur without any conscious reflection about different choices that might lead to different outcomes. In conflict situations, the last thing most people consider is the possibility of transforming conflict into collaboration for the purpose of creating a peaceful outcome. There is simply nothing instinctive about this, so our choices tend to follow the natural course of opposition.

The remaining three pillars of healing and peace—thinking, feeling, and behavior—each require the carving of new paths in the forest of your subconscious mind. Each will require effort, repetition, and time to become well-established, familiar, and routinely used. And each will, to some extent, be examples of going against the habits of your mind's more familiar and automatic ways of thinking, feeling, and behaving. The subconscious mind is a creature of habit that will always favor what is automatic and known versus what is new and unknown. It has little interest in the creation of new paths and will naturally favor the tried and true. Therefore, in order to get these new paths opened up, well-established, and eventually part of your second nature, the influence of repeated intention will be necessary (just as when you may have first learned to ride a bike or swim).

When hikers get lost in the woods, their most natural inclination is to hike downhill, expecting that this direction will eventually lead them to safety. However, the instinct to descend to lower terrain when lost may be counterproductive and get one lost in deeper canyons or valleys. This can leave hikers without any bearings on where they are or in what direction to proceed. Instead, if they were to climb uphill to a point allowing a clearer vantage point, the chances for finding the best route are greatly improved. Having the intention to get a clearer vantage point can lead to choosing a better route uphill rather than following the more natural inclination to go downhill. In conflict situations, having the intention of peace will lead you in directions counter to your natural instincts. It's equivalent to pulling out your compass and choosing a direction toward peace, and then taking the new paths you have created in that direction.

The adoption of the intention to pursue healing and peace is the simplest of all the five pillars to adopt, but it's also one of the most influential. In the woods, you may not be able to find an easy path to climb uphill, but simply knowing that you should go uphill could be what makes all the difference in rescuing yourself. *The intention of healing and peace will need to be chosen again and again by your conscious mind before it will become more familiar and automatic for your subconscious mind to choose on its own.* The more you can make this your intention, the sooner healing and peace will become a greater part of your life.

CHAPTER 6

Thinking

Carving out new paths for thinking your way toward healing and peace has less to do with *what* you think than learning *how to think differently*. Specifically, there are three alternative ways to think differently that serve these purposes well. I refer to these thinking patterns as 1) "rainbow" thinking, 2) reflective thinking, and 3) Golden Rule thinking. These thinking styles are nothing new, but rather are being referred to with this terminology for greater clarity.

Rainbow Thinking

Rainbow thinking is a term intended to contrast with black-and-white thinking. Rainbow thinking and black-and-white thinking are two ways of attempting to understand the world and the nature of reality. These thinking styles result in entirely different perceptions, which in turn influence feelings and behaviors in profoundly different ways. Consider the following comparisons.

Black-and-white thinking tends to be simple, clear, certain, and primitive. By contrast, rainbow thinking is more complex, ambiguous, uncertain, and evolved. Instead of perceiving reality as divided between black and white opposites, rainbow thinking perceives a wide spectrum of different colored realities capable of overlapping, blending with one another, and creating a wider range of realities, just like the colors of a rainbow do. Black-and-white thinking polarizes reality into a series of opposites (dualism), such as right and wrong, good and bad, or us and them, in ways that are absolute and divisive. Rainbow thinking allows for the recognition and integration of multiple differences in ways that are not fundamentally divisive. Instead, it recognizes how different colors all belong on the spectrum of light.

Black-and-white thinking leads to reactions of certainty, conviction, judgment, fear, hostility, and hatred, all of which intensify adversity and conflict. Rainbow thinking results in reactions of understanding, empathy, acceptance, and inclusiveness that promote conditions for healing, peace, and harmony. Black-and-white thinking is a *reactive* style of thinking that narrows the range of choices perceived. Rainbow thinking is a more *reflective*, analytical style of thinking that lends itself to more complete information processing, such as the ability to view things from more than one perspective.

Lastly, black-and-white thinking occurs in the lower, more primitive regions of the brain that make up the limbic system (hippocampus, amygdala, and hypothalamus). Rainbow thinking takes place in the higher, more evolved region of the brain known as the cerebral cortex.

Dualistic beliefs that promote black-and-white thinking lead down paths that promote greater opposition, conflict, and aggression. Monistic beliefs that promote rainbow thinking lead down paths that promote greater understanding, integration, healing, and peace. Together, these belief systems and styles of thinking determine how we perceive and relate to others with whom we experience conflict.

Reflective Thinking

The contrast between *reflective* thinking and *reactive* thinking can be recognized in the following situation. Imagine a young child playing with a ball that accidentally rolls out of the yard and across the street. The child's most natural and immediate instinct would be to chase after the ball without pausing to consider the possibility of traffic coming from either direction. This version of reactive thinking could endanger the child's life. A more mature child would possess the advanced cognitive capacity to pause and look in both directions before pursuing the ball, and this example of reflective thinking would allow the child to both retrieve the ball and remain alive.

Reflective thinking is more proactive and open-minded than reactive thinking, which is more impulsive in nature. Reflective thinking has us look more carefully before we leap to conclusions, judgment, and action. Reactive thinking is more knee-jerk or trigger-happy in nature. It does not take extra time for data gathering and analysis before arriving at conclusions, judgments, and action. Reactive thinking is controlled by the programs of the subconscious mind, thereby bypassing conscious reflection. Reflective thinking first requires an inhibition of these subconscious impulses to then give the analytical cortex the chance to complete its homework. Reflective thinking is more accurate for discerning a fuller truth, making better judgments, and making wiser behavioral choices because it benefits from a synthesis of multiple perspectives. Uninhibited reactive thinking may be easier, faster, and more certain than reflexive thinking, but, because it's less complete, it's more likely to result in mistakes that perpetuate conflict.

There are other ways in which reflective thinking is essential for making better choices in life. Our minds all have distortions built into the lenses (subconscious biases) through which we perceive the world. Some people are known for wearing rose-colored glasses that make them see the world in more optimistic and naive ways, while others may view the world through the lens of cynicism. Some learn to automatically look for threats and danger in their environments while others look for opportunities. There are countless different lenses that bias our perceptions of the world in both favorable and unfavorable ways, and most people are unaware of their biases because they are programmed into the subconscious.

Socrates' famous dictum, "The unexamined life is not worth living," promoted the value of reflective thinking through logical analysis and argument. But Socrates went even further with his directive to "know thyself," indicating that there are limitations in one's ability to examine and understand the outside world unless one's inner world was examined as well. Learning how to reflect on how your own mind functions can help you to discover the distorted lenses and biases that shape your perceptions of the outer world. This can be difficult to do independently, which is why you may need family, friends, teachers, or therapists to help you look in the mirror for them. Reflective thinking is most beneficial when it's applied to both your outer world and inner self.

Golden Rule Thinking

Golden Rule thinking represents a style of thinking that provides the key to empathy. Empathy is the cognitive and emotional process that allows us to understand and feel the experiences of others. It requires a thinking style that puts us into the shoes of other people in ways that help us understand their perceptions, thoughts, emotions, and needs. Some people can do this quite naturally and easily, but it's not as universal as reactive thinking. Fortunately, Golden Rule thinking skills can be acquired through practice until they become easier and more natural to use in everyday life.

In order to use Golden Rule thinking to achieve accurate empathic understandings of others, it's necessary to suspend black-and-white judgmental thinking. This is because judgmental thinking closes the mind to new ways of understanding others. In place of judgment, one must activate an open-minded curiosity to understand what makes other people tick. Such curiosity may require various measures of active inquiry, reflective thinking, and sometimes imagination, as in, "I wonder what it would be like if I was in their shoes?" This type of thinking is also far more advanced than reactive black-and-white thinking. It takes more time and effort, and is therefore a very caring labor. We all know what it's like to feel misunderstood by others and to wish they would make the effort to put themselves in our shoes. If this is what we would like others to do for us, then it makes sense for us to offer it to others as well.

Golden Rule thinking is another example of the need to develop new pathways of thinking in the forest of the mind. People with highly advanced versions of this ability can often understand what it's like inside of others within moments of interacting with them. For most people this requires a conscious effort, however the more one engages in Golden Rule thinking, the easier it becomes, even reaching the point where it may become part of your second nature.

CHAPTER 7

Feelings

There are some very effective emotional tools that can help bring about healing and peace within yourself and between yourself and others. Empathy and compassion are the most powerful of these emotional tools.

The more you practice Golden Rule thinking to understand the experiences of others, the more this will develop your feelings of empathy and compassion. These feelings will not be enough to resolve conflict, but they will be enormously helpful for managing conflicts more effectively. For instance, when your mind is engaged in Golden Rule thinking to help you empathize with others, you'll find yourself becoming less judgmental of the different positions and values they hold. Because judgment only intensifies conflict, replacing it with empathy and compassion will have the opposite effect.

A second benefit of cultivating empathy and compassion toward others is that these feelings can be very effective at helping others to become more calm. Better still, once others feel the reassuring benefits

31

of your empathy, they become much more likely to respond to you with empathic consideration of your positions and values. One of the strongest social codes programmed into the human subconscious has to do with reciprocity. This principle is more familiarly known as "tit-for-tat" or "what goes around comes around." Because this instinct applies equally to both kind and unkind behaviors, you can activate empathic kindness in others by offering it to them first.

Here's another way to understand the importance of controlling your feelings when in conflict. The greater the perceived threat, the more the stress hormones of adrenaline and cortisol are released, priming our bodies for fight or flight. These chemicals disturb one's inner peace, impair the ability to think clearly, and reduce the odds for healthy conflict resolutions. Therefore it's not only beneficial to control the body chemistry of fear and aggression, but it's much better to activate the body chemistry associated with empathy and compassion – namely, oxytocin. When either party in a conflict is able to do this, an opportunity is created for the other party to follow suit. Someone just needs to take the lead, so you might as well learn to develop this skill yourself. This is an integral part of the process of transforming oppositional dynamics into collaborative ones.

Consider this metaphor to understand what a critical difference emotions can make in a threatening situation. Imagine that your rational mind is the pilot of your plane. When your plane finds itself on a collision course with another plane, this might cause your pilot to become overwhelmed by the chemistry of fear or anger in relation to the other plane. If your pilot is not able to subdue these feelings, they may impair its judgment, and thereby endanger your well-being. The same would be the case for the pilot of the other plane. In order for both pilots and their passengers to navigate through the conflict safely, they would be well-served to recognize their shared interest in survival. Any communications between the pilots would require an exchange of respect, information, understanding, and the good will to work together toward a successful resolution of the conflict. In many conflict situations, the healthiest resolutions will be facilitated by the presence of more caring emotional attitudes.

Conjuring the positive emotional experiences of empathy and compassion in the midst of conflict is neither easy nor natural for most people because it's the complete opposite emotional experience of fear and anger. The subconscious mind will automatically favor the paths of fight or flight under these circumstances, so training your mind to use the paths of empathy and compassion will require plenty of practice and time before it becomes another part of your second nature.

CHAPTER 8

Behavior

The first four pillars of healing and peace – belief, intention, thinking, and feeling – together pave the way for the fifth pillar of healing, *behavior*. This pillar can be broken down into four essentials:

1. Collaboration
2. Nurturance
3. Integration
4. Healing

Collaboration

Remember that conflict situations naturally activate the oppositional instincts of fight or flight, neither of which leads to healing and peace. The alternative to opposition is collaboration. Converting oppositional dynamics into collaboration is one of the most important keys for conflict management.

In conflicts with others, you want to learn how to go from working *against* to working *with*. The more you employ the skills of Golden Rule thinking to cultivate understanding, empathy, and compassion, the more you will be fostering collaboration with others. This reduces antagonism and competition and helps offset the influence of stress hormones in both parties.

The specifics of the collaborative process include the effort to understand the position of others, combined with the effort to help others understand your own position; in other words, working *with* one another to understand one another. From there, collaboration can proceed toward exploring and negotiating compromises and agreements. Effective conflict management is undermined by oppositional paths, and enhanced by collaborative paths.

Nurturance

The purpose of nurturance in the context of conflict is to transform discomfort into comfort. The four essential elements of emotional nurturance for the purpose of conflict management are:

1. Understanding
2. Empathy
3. Acceptance
4. Reassurance

There are other elements of nurturance such as attention, affection, warmth, appreciation, praise, validation, and affirmation that serve other purposes, but the four enumerated above will be highlighted for their value in conflict management.

Understanding

There are four valuable lessons to learn about the importance of understanding. The most important of these is that understanding is a very effective tool for soothing discomfort and easing tensions in conflict situations. The second lesson is that understanding will benefit the party that is gaining new understanding. It's not possible to find effective remedies unless a problem is properly understood first. Third, understanding eases tension in conflict situations. The understood party is calmed by feeling understood, and the understanding party is better able to release judgments based upon misunderstandings. This is even more true when understanding can be exchanged in both directions. Each party feels less threatened when understood by the other, and this helps prepare the way for managing conflict more effectively. Parties that understand one another become much more willing to collaborate and compromise to resolve their conflicts. The fourth lesson about understanding is that it's often most helpful when separated from immediate efforts to solve problems. Men are especially eager to fix things, and this all too often leads to either skipping the efforts to understand problems adequately, or else moving too quickly from understanding to problem solving. It's better to let understanding have an opportunity to sink in before launching into fix-it mode. Let the heart have a chance to settle before engaging the rational part of your mind.

Empathy

Empathy has already been described as the ability to put oneself into the shoes of another, and to accurately sense what the other person is feeling in those shoes. Empathy, combined with understanding, helps to connect both the mind and the heart of others, further magnifying the dynamics of collaboration.

Imagine that you have a terrible illness that's causing you great confusion and emotional distress. You find a brilliant doctor who is able to diagnose the illness and explain its meaning to you, which provides some measure of reassurance. But what if your doctor conveyed this information in entirely rational terms without any regard for your emotional distress? Now, imagine getting a second opinion from another doctor who agrees with everything the first doctor explained, but conveys an empathic awareness for how frightened you are as well. The first doctor may have brought comfort to your mind, but the second doctor may bring greater comfort to you because s/he is addressing both your mind and your heart. Even though both doctors may be equally competent to treat your illness, you might prefer to be treated by the doctor who demonstrates care for your feelings, not just your body. In other words, you may be more motivated to work *with* the doctor who both understands and cares empathically. This same principle applies to our willingness to work through conflicts with others.

Acceptance

When in conflict with others, expressions of acceptance have the opposite effect from condemning judgments. Judgments feel threatening; acceptance is calming and therefore another key element of nurturing. When combined with expressions of understanding and empathy, an attitude of acceptance for the "other" who holds a contrasting position is very disarming. To say something like, "I get and accept where you're coming from," is not the same as offering agreement, but it is immensely comforting. We can accept others and still disagree with their opinion or position on a matter. Taking judgment out of the equation and replacing it with acceptance is essential for minimizing opposition. This allows distressed minds to relax their defense mechanisms. When both parties feel accepted, cooler heads can then move forward more comfortably toward collaborative conflict management.

Reassurance

Reassurance follows understanding, empathy, and acceptance with comforting messages such as:

- "It will be alright."
- "We'll find a way to figure this out."
- "I'm willing to compromise with you."
- "Why don't we make a deal?"

Reassuring comments like these provide simple, yet important, reinforcement for the spirit of goodwill, acceptance, collaboration, and the intention to make peace.

Integration

Conflict is a divisive experience. The opposite of division is integration. When you apply Golden Rule thinking to the process of collaborating with others, you are beginning the transition from division to integration. The first stage of integration in conflict is the integration of wills. When parents are in conflict with one another over how to discipline their children, this creates an unstable confusion that undermines the effectiveness of discipline and creates strife that impacts the entire family. There are many different styles of parenting that can be highly effective, but they all rely on an integrated, united front between parents to work best for the child's interests. Otherwise, the conditions for divide-and-conquer manipulations exist for children to exploit.

The integration of will does not automatically resolve conflict, however the chances for resolving conflict are maximized exponentially when two wills are combining to search for conflict resolutions. Consider the difference made when two political parties in congress refuse to collaborate or compromise with one another for purely ideological reasons. Such intractable stand-offs fail to produce any effective governance, and have even been known to shut government operations down altogether. But when opposing political parties establish a willingness to work together to govern, even though their differences remain, compromise solutions will be found to solve the problems they were elected to address.

On whatever scale conflict exists, within an individual, a marriage, a family, a government, or between nations, disagreements will be more peacefully managed when an integration of wills can be established first. Children can grow up peacefully with parents who have conflicts with one another, provided that the children recognize a fundamental integration of their parents wills that helps them work through their differences together. They will be able to trust when their parents offer them the reassurance, "Don't worry, Mommy and Daddy can work this out together."

Healing

Converting conflict into peace can be a challenge even under ideal circumstances. When unhealed emotional wounds exist in either or both parties in a conflict, reaching peace is even more challenging. Under these circumstances, the five pillars of healing and peace will be of less benefit until wounds are healed first. These may be wounds caused by a current conflict, or wounds that were caused many years earlier. Either way, emotional wounds can interfere with the emotional calm necessary to think clearly, empathize accurately, and trust others in the ways necessary to manage conflict effectively.

The subject of healing requires a book of its own, but the basics for healing are relatively simple to grasp. Here is a list of some of the most essential elements for emotional healing to occur:

- Understanding
- Empathy, respect, and compassion
- Reassurance
- Behavior change
- Forgiveness
- Renewal of trust and confidence

You will recognize the overlap between the elements of conflict management and those of the healing process. This is because what is being addressed in both is some form of relationship process, either within oneself or with others.

Emotional wounds involve some form of breakdown in trust and/or confidence in oneself or others. A range of painful emotions may enter this gap, such as fear, sadness, despair, humiliation, guilt, shame, anger, or hatred. For emotional wounds to heal, they must first be cleansed of the toxic emotions occupying that wounded space. Because these wounds are areas of great emotional vulnerability, healing them can only occur under the conditions of utmost safety and care. Sometimes, this may involve the person who caused or contributed to the wound, though often the healing process may need to begin privately with someone skilled in the healing process. Again, this might involve a family member, close friend, spiritual counselor, or a therapist. Part 4 of this book will address how emotional healing can be pursued independently or with others.

Here is a concise description of how the elements listed above contribute to the healing of emotional wounds. The first step is for the nature and the cause of the wound to be clearly understood. This may require lengthy periods of reflection and dialogue in order to get to the heart of the matter. This can only take place successfully when undertaken in a trustworthy context that is free from judgment. Accurate understanding needs to be accompanied by empathy, respect, and compassion for the wounded person's experience. Together, these attributes make it possible for emotional wounds to become more accessible to the healing process. This is analogous to unwrapping protective bandages in preparation for cleansing and repairing a physical wound.

After an emotional wound has been accessed with understanding, empathy, respect, and compassion, it next needs to be cleansed. This may require grieving and forgiveness, both of which are delicate experiences. The forgiveness required may (or may not) need to be directed toward those who have caused or contributed to the wound, however there may also need to be forgiveness of oneself.

Consider the emotional wounds associated with sexual assault. These wounds are capable of leaving behind the toxic emotions of both hatred and shame, either of which can fester and interfere with healing forever. This is not to suggest that sexual assault victims should ever be expected to forgive their perpetrators. Abuse victims can only decide for themselves if and when offering forgiveness will benefit their inner healing or the healing of relationships with loved-ones who may have harmed them. Either way, when sexual assault leaves behind the toxins of shame (victims are commonly left with greater feelings of shame than their perpetrators are), then these feelings need to be released through a process of self-forgiveness. Such complex and intense challenges often require the expert guidance of a professional therapist. Letting go of hatred and shame can go a long way toward healing emotional wounds and restoring greater levels of peace in the wake of such traumas.

In order to assist the process of forgiving others who have caused emotional wounds, genuine expressions of remorse, apology, and assurances of behavior change are often necessary. These cannot be empty words (insincere) or merely words alone. In order for forgiveness and healing to be as full as possible, true behavioral change must also be demonstrated and sustained over time.

Summary

The behavioral elements for converting conflict back into healing and peace consist of collaboration, nurturance, integration, and healing. Together, they represent the fifth pillar of healing and peace, and are dependent upon the combined support of the other four pillars – belief, intention, thinking, and feeling. These five pillars of healing and peace do not come pre-programmed in your subconscious mind the way the more basic instincts for survival do. Together, they represent a new program to be acquired and practiced for managing conflict and creating more wholeness in your life.

CHAPTER 9

The Relationship Between Inner and Outer Healing and Peace

The five pillars of healing and peace – belief, intention, thinking, feeling, and behavior, have been introduced in the context of how the operating system of the mind can be upgraded to create more healing and peace with others. Yet this is only half of the story about the path to healing and peace. The more important half of the story has to do with the need to apply these pillars toward creating healing and peace within yourself. If you are lacking these within yourself, this will impose limits on the degree of peace and intimacy you can enjoy with others in your life. What does it mean to be lacking inner peace and wholeness? It means that you have unresolved conflicts and wounds within your mind. And the reason this is possible is because your personality is made up of multiple contrasting parts, and these parts frequently end up in conflict with one another. That's right, there are "others" inhabiting your subconscious mind, and they need help with the conflicts that exist between them. This reality has several very important implications.

The first implication is that how you perceive and relate to other people is heavily influenced by how the different parts of your subconscious mind interact with one another. In <u>Creed</u>, the final chapter of the famous Rocky movies, Rocky (Sylvester Stallone) plays the wise mentor to his young boxing protégé, Adonis Creed. In one scene, Rocky poses young Adonis in front of a full-length mirror and explains to him that his reflected image is the most important opponent he needs to learn to fight with, both in the ring and in the real world. This wisdom captures the idea that your relationship with the world is a reflection of your relationship with yourself. The correspondence between your inner and outer relationships is not an exact one, but where you have conflicts within yourself will be mirrored in the conflicts you have with others.

The second implication of the correspondence between your inner and outer worlds is that the same set of skills for cultivating healing and peace with outer conflicts works for resolving inner conflicts as well. This means that using the five pillars to make healing and peace with others will help prepare you for making healing and peace within yourself, and using them to make peace within your mind will better prepare you for transforming relationships with others. "As within, so without"; it works in both directions.

The third implication of the mirror realities of inner and outer conflicts is that by examining your conflicts in the world you can gain insight into where you may need to heal and make peace within yourself. For instance, if you repeatedly find yourself in conflict with authority figures in your life, this may indicate that you have some form of conflict with your own inner authority. Or, if you find yourself intolerant and judgmental toward people who you perceive as vulnerable, this may suggest that you have a conflict with the vulnerable sides of your own nature. More will be explained about the nature of your subpersonalities in part 2 of the book. The conflicts between these inner subpersonalities will also be described in greater detail.

The final implication of the mirror realities of your inner and outer world is that the best way to create healing and peace in your life is to begin by healing the wounds and conflicts within yourself first. Because most types of conflict in the outer world will have a mirror version within your subconscious, learning to peacefully integrate the conflicting parts within yourself will automatically make it easier for you to manage conflict with others. The familiar adage, "You are your own worst enemy," precisely captures this point. Once you can learn how to stop being your own worst enemy, you'll discover that you'll end up with far fewer enemies in your life.

PART II

A Model of the Mind

CHAPTER 10

Who Do You Think You Are?

What is it that defines who you are as a person? Certainly it's more than being a daughter, son, husband, wife, mother, father, or your occupational status or role in life. Your identity is largely defined by your values and the things you care about the most, and these are things that often change as we develop throughout childhood, adolescence, adulthood, and maturity. The question of your identity is a complex question because identities are *complexes* themselves.

A complex is a collection of interconnected structures that are organized by their relationships to one another. In any complex, there is both a shared identity and a set of separate identities. The independent identities in a structure may be extremely different from one another, like the different ethnic groups populating a city. The overall identity of a city would be defined not just by the sum of its individual parts, but also by how its inhabitants interacted with one another. For instance, two identical cities might both have an array of different ethnic groups populating them, but if the relationships between those ethnic groups in one city was hostile, and those in the other were civil, then the two cities would have very different characters. Likewise, your identity is a collection of different parts that can relate to one another in different ways, and your personality is largely determined by how those parts interact with one another. Furthermore, how your parts interact internally will have a large influence on how you interact with other people.

The individual parts that form your identity exist to serve separate functions, and these functions all have their unique sets of values. For instance, your conscience serves to guide your behavior in order to keep you out of trouble and in the good graces of your social and work groups. To do so it must value the rules, ethics, and morals that the group shares for behaving appropriately with one another. In contrast to your conscience would be your sexual identity, with its function to pursue pleasure, intimacy and possibly procreation. Therefore it will value attractiveness, health, and behaviors that serve attraction, pleasure and procreation best. If you have children (or plan to), then parts of you will need to serve the functions of protection, nurturance, discipline, and education, and each of these functions will be associated with different sets of values.

The sciences of neuroanatomy and neuropsychology have shed a lot of light on how the brain functions in specialized and localized ways, as well as in more unified and interconnected ways. One theory brought to light by these disciplines is known as "functional specialization," or "modularity." These terms represent the notion that specific functions of the mature mind are localized in specific "modules" of the brain, and there is an abundance of scientific evidence in support of this model of brain functioning. At the same time, there are so many exceptions to this rule that a complementary theory known as "distributive processing" has developed in order to explain how multiple sites in the brain collaborate simultaneously in processing information. In other words, different parts of the brain are specialized for different purposes, but they also work together as a team to accomplish an endless variety of complex tasks that no specialized region of the brain can perform on its own.

The parceling of the mind into different parts is nothing new. Sigmund Freud, the father of psychoanalytic theory, was among the first to popularize the notion that our psyches are made up of different parts, which he designated as the ego, id, and superego. Freud provided explanations for these functions and how emotional problems were commonly the result of conflicts between them. Other schools of psychodynamic theory followed shortly thereafter, with each establishing their own classification systems for the various parts of the psyche and their complex interactions with one another.

Following Freud, there have been numerous other models for the makeup of our intrapsychic families. In the late 1950s, psychiatrist Eric Berne developed a popular alternative known as Transactional Analysis (TA) which identified *Parent, Adult,* and *Child* "ego states" to characterize the different parts of the mind. This model had many obvious parallels to the Freudian model in that an authoritative Parent structure was required to regulate immature Child instincts, and a more rational Adult was necessary to mediate the conflicts between them. The most popular model today of the multiplicity of the mind's nature was developed by Dr. Richard Schwartz. Schwartz's Internal Family System (IFS) theory breaks the psyche down into groups of subpersonalities along the following lines:

- "Managers" are responsible for protecting oneself from conflicts with the outside world and from internal sources of pain.
- "Exiles" represent internal sources of pain (grief, fear, shame, and trauma) formed from childhood wounds.
- "Firefighters" are a collection of defense mechanisms that spring into action when the emotional exiles get out of control.

- "Self" is considered the spiritual center of the personality that possesses the capabilities of healing the wounds and conflicts that exist between the other parts.

Most recently, the highly popular Pixar movie, <u>Inside Out,</u> offers a fine depiction of how a 12-year-old girl's personality is controlled by the characters *Anger, Disgust, Joy, Fear,* and *Sadness,* who work inside her brain's headquarters.

More important than deciding how to label the mind's sub-personalities is the recognition that we are all made up of multiple contrasting parts that conflict with one another, and which therefore require some form of regulation. Of even greater importance than the nature of these parts is the type of program used to govern their interactions with one another.

In order to understand this concept of regulating multiple parts more clearly, let's use a musical metaphor. Imagine a group of talented and motivated musicians meeting and getting acquainted for the first time. The group has no identity yet because they haven't even decided what type of music to play. This decision won't occur until some form of leader (a conductor) can organize the players and help them determine how they'll be making music together as a group. No matter how much individual and collective talent exists in this group, it will not be able to produce anything harmonious unless they can be led to work together as a whole. Without a leader, there will be chaotic noises resulting from conflict and competition between different factions of musicians. There's nothing wrong with an orchestra or band playing different types of music for different audiences under different circumstances. What will define the identity of the group will be whether it performs music harmoniously or chaotically. The same is true of one's identity and personality.

Just as every complex group of musicians needs a gifted conductor to bring out their best harmonies, every individual needs some type of internal conductor to perform this organizing function internally. Freud gave the label of Ego to the conductor in his psychoanalytic model. Berne's conductor in TA was the Adult, and Schwartz's IFS conductor is the Self. Whatever you want to call the conducting function of the intrapsychic family, that part needs to have a program for managing conflicting functions and values in order to maximize harmony and wholeness. This program is informed by our values and goals.

There is no consensus on the number of subpersonalities or specialized modules in the mind, nor is there any consensus on how these parts should be labeled. What is most valuable to understand about the nature of the mind is that it is indeed made up of a variety of separate parts that have separate functions, and these parts can either conflict with one another or work together. It's equally important to understand that individuals can exert influence on how the different parts of their mind work, and by learning how to exert this influence, people can change the course of their lives.

The classification system that will be introduced in chapter 11, "Cast of Characters," is one that has evolved over the past 25 years in my own practice. It borrows from and overlaps with other classifications systems that have paved the way for it, and there is very little about it that makes it any better than its predecessors. The biggest difference it introduces is an alternate interpretation of the function of the conductor(s). But any model that attempts to classify different parts of the mind is of little value in the absence of a system for orchestrating the interactions between these different parts. Without a systematic program performing this function, the subconscious mind functions according to the operating system that it inherited at birth and that was subsequently modified throughout childhood. That leaves out any influence that an individual might want to introduce after reaching the age of reason (the adult capacity for critical thinking). All too often these inherited operating systems in the subconscious are full of limitations and myths that perpetuate conflict more than peace.

Rationally thinking adults may believe that they have complete conscious control over their lives, but that would be overlooking the extraordinary influence of the *non*-rational subconscious mind. What Socrates meant by saying, "The unexamined life is not worth living," was that we need to be more conscious of these internal influences that are ordinarily hidden from our awareness. Otherwise we will suffer from the unregulated conflicts occurring between different parts in the subconscious, as well as conflicts between the conscious and subconscious layers of the mind.

CHAPTER 11

A Cast of Characters

This chapter will attempt to provide a map of the subconscious mind. This will not be an exact or complete map of the subconscious because the mind is not as easily mapped out as the physical brain is. But to understand the general idea of how the subconscious mind works does not require a precise knowledge of its contents. Identical twins with the same brains, if raised under extremely different circumstances, could end up with extremely different minds. While not all minds are alike, there are some universal functions that they all share, as well as some common dynamics that influence how these functions interact.

I find it helpful to regard the subconscious mind as consisting of two fundamental layers or depths. The primary layer that will receive the most attention in this book will be described as consisting of eight core subpersonalities. A secondary layer that lies deeper in the mind and less accessible to conscious awareness is referred to as the Shadow, a term coined by Freud's contemporary, Carl Jung, in 1912. This chapter, and the following one, will focus on the workings of the primary layer of the subconscious; the secondary layer of the shadow will receive separate attention in chapter 13. There are two reasons for this separation in treatment of these layers, one having to do with sequence and another having to do with complexity. The conflicts and wounds existing in the shadow layer of the subconscious are best addressed only once the conflicts and wounds in the primary layer of the subconscious are first addressed. Working with the eight core subpersonalities in this first layer will not only provide an important foundation in preparation for subsequently exploring the shadow terrain, but this first layer will be the best place to learn the process of healing and integration which creates healing and peace for the mind. The shadow layer is where deeper and more complex wounds and conflicts exist in the psyche, and therefore is associated with greater risk. Healing and integration at this level exceeds the scope of this book, though it will be presented because everything else in this book is fundamental for those who may need to eventually pursue healing there at some later time (and with the professional assistance that would be recommended for that).

Function versus Method

Before offering descriptions of each of these subpersonalities, it's important to understand that each one has both a *function* (purpose) and a *method* for serving its function. For instance, the Judge serves functions related to controlling your behavior and that of others for whom you may have responsibility (children/employees). However, there are many different methods of exercising controlling authority. There are some police officers who rely on a stern, intimidating method for enforcing the law, while other officers may rely on a more courteous, yet firm method of enforcement. This distinction between function and method is important because oftentimes a valuable function becomes undone by the use of a poor method.

If this distinction isn't understood clearly, certain functions may be devalued simply because of the poor methods used to serve that function (throwing the baby out with the bathwater). If the police in a city employed overly harsh methods of law enforcement, you wouldn't want the city to eliminate the police force. You would want to retain the value of a police force and have them retrained to use better methods for performing their function.

As you become more acquainted with the various parts of your mind, you will inevitably discover things you don't like about these parts. When you do, it will be important to understand that it's the method that is the problem, not the function itself. You'll want to understand and embrace that part's functions, while considering how you may need to modify its method.

A second reason that you may have concerns about your different parts is because, like every coin, there are two sides to their nature. Think of these two sides as the *virtue* side and the *curse* side, referring to the fact that every part of your nature has its own advantages and disadvantages. These will be explained about each subpersonality as they are introduced.

The remainder of this chapter is devoted to an introduction of the eight core subpersonalities that most people will be easily able to recognize within themselves as they function on a daily basis. These are:

1. The Heart
2. The Judge
3. The Nurturer
4. The Warrior
5. The Ego
6. The Rebel
7. The Romantic
8. The Sexual Self

The Heart

This is a reference to the emotional heart of your nature, not to your physical heart. Many self-help authors, educators, and therapists will refer to the Heart as the *Inner Child,* which is perfectly fine. The only important point to keep in mind about the term Inner Child is that it's not referring to your childhood, but rather to your deepest level of emotional sensitivity as it exists throughout the lifespan. The Heart represents emotional vulnerability and need. Maturing into rational adulthood does not mean eliminating this part of our nature, although we often learn to conceal it better from others and even ourselves.

Your Heart, just like any child, has two fundamental and contrasting needs. The first is for safety, and the second is for love and affection. These terms are broad and can mean a lot of different things, but what is important to understand is that these two fundamental needs exist *in conflict* with one another. In order for your Heart to feel safe, it must be guarded in some way, which imposes limits on its ability to exchange love and affection openly. In order for your Heart to enjoy the benefits of love and affection, it must be open, accessible, and capable of exchanging caring feelings with others, which leaves it more vulnerable to the pains of loss, rejection, betrayal, judgment, and hostility.

In order for your Heart to enjoy maximum peace, these conflicting needs must be adequately met and balanced so that love and affection can be exchanged with others in safe, protected ways. This may sound simple, but accomplishing this balance requires a great deal of maturity and skill; in other words, a well regulated operating system for the mind.

The virtue side of the Heart's coin is that it will guide you toward love, happiness, and peace if you learn how to listen to it and meet its needs. The curse side of the Heart is that it can be so sensitive and vulnerable that it will expose you to great miseries. These miseries can become so intolerable that many people will look for ways to close their Hearts, harden them, or deaden them with alcohol and drugs. This is an example of throwing the baby out with the bathwater. In order to enjoy the virtues of the Heart, its need for protection from the curses of emotional misery must be balanced and integrated with the opportunities for love and affection.

The Judge

The Judge is like the inner parent that maintains responsibility and authority for controlling and directing your life. The concept is roughly equivalent to Freud's Superego, Berne's Parent ego state, or more commonly understood as a person's conscience. The Judge must learn the rules of society and ensure that you conform to the codes necessary to keep you out of trouble. This means regulating your impulses and temptations, while also driving you in directions that will earn approval, achievement, and reward from others.

The Judge's functions are by no means simple or easy. Among other things, it must regulate the desires of your Sexual Self, the competitiveness of your Ego, the provocations of your Rebel, the follies of your Heart and Romantic, and the aggression of your Warrior. All too often a Judge may assume the characteristics of an overbearing tyrant in its desperation to keep things under control, causing great harm to one's peace and self-esteem in the process.

The character of your Judge is the byproduct of both your biology and your upbringing (nature and nurture). It began getting programmed in early childhood before your brain's higher faculties of reasoning developed. Because of this developmental sequence, your Judge's code of *shoulds* and *shouldn'ts* may not always be reasonable. The Judge internalizes rules and standards imposed by governing authorities (parents, teachers, cultural norms, religious leaders). Because a Judge's codes are adopted based on trust in influential authorities, the codes may never be questioned or challenged through independent reflection. Such codes are often rigidly held and impervious to rational argument or contradictory evidence. This is not to say that a Judge's codes are impossible to modify, but that modifying them requires accessing the subconscious part of the mind and using other forms of persuasion to encourage change.

The virtue of the Judge is that it navigates you through life like the captain of a ship, steering you away from danger and toward your desired destination. The curse side of the Judge is that it has the power to make you feel absolutely terrible about yourself in the process. Oftentimes a Judge's principal tool for exercising its influence is through the use of intense guilt, shame, criticism, condemnation, and other forms of mental punishment. In extreme cases, this can lead to crippling anxiety, depression, or even suicide.

The Nurturer

The Nurturer is the Judge's co-director of the intrapsychic family. Unfortunately, the influence of the Nurturer is frequently inactive or overshadowed by the dominance of the Judge. That does not mean that your Nurturer is undeveloped or inert. Many big-hearted individuals have extremely gifted nurturing capabilities, however they tend to be directed more toward others than toward oneself. Such caregivers provide effective comfort to children, spouses, the elderly, patients, and others in need, yet may not have learned how to nurture themselves in kind. Such selflessness and sacrifice may seem virtuous, but can eventually result in emotional exhaustion and resentment. When this happens, the Nurturer must learn to assume greater responsibility for meeting the needs of the Heart (and body), and the Judge needs to allow for this to happen. The Judge's permission for this is necessary because frequently *self-care* becomes confused with *selfishness*, which is something that may go against the Judge's code. Self-nurturance is not selfishness. Instead, it's what is necessary in order for caregivers to refill their own emotional tanks and regain physical energy so that they can continue being effective caregivers to others.

Emotional nurturance provides attention, empathy, understanding, compassion, and reassurance to Hearts in distress. These gifts are useful not only for providing comfort, but for emotional healing also. These are the obvious virtues of the Nurturer. There are two curses on the other side of the Nurturer's coin. The first is when a Nurturer neglects the necessity of control in favor of comfort, such as when a parent may fail to discipline a child for fear of hurting the child's feelings or self-esteem (and thereby spoil him/her). Such enabling behaviors weakens children and does them a disservice. The second curse is the mistake of being too self-sacrificing, as mentioned above. This is the hazard that all airline safety instructions address prior to takeoff. For those passengers traveling with children or other dependents, in the event of an emergency they are directed to place the oxygen mask on themselves prior to assisting their dependents.

The Nurturer is another dimension of the human heart, however it's the side of the heart that is capable of *giving* care, in contrast to the Inner Child/Heart which is the side in need of *receiving* care.

The Warrior

The Warrior is your guardian and protector. Your Warrior is a source of power that serves to set and enforce limits on those who threaten you or your loved ones in some way. Its powers include the use of anger, aggression, and violence if necessary.

Like our nation's warriors who serve in the military, our police forces, firefighters, and other civil protectors, your own inner Warrior embodies the virtues of courage and devotion to your safety. Whenever it senses that your Heart, body, or other interest is in some form of danger, the Warrior may spring into action with lightning speed. These are all virtues that make our Warriors heroic. The curse side of the Warrior is its vulnerability to impulsivity and use of excessive force. As valuable as it is to have an effective defense system, the overuse of force can actually worsen your overall security. Dominant aggression is often a fuel for resentment and deepening hostilities, sowing the seeds of potential rebellion or vindictiveness from others in response. Overpowering others will often harm relationships with them, thereby eroding both your long-term security and peace. Therefore, the use of defensive power must be measured and judicious in order to be most effective.

The Ego

In order to properly introduce the Ego, a clarification in terminology is required. The Ego subpersonality being referred to here is not the same as Freud's ego. The term ego has long held two separate meanings in popular usage. Freud's version referred to the reasonable function of the mind that mediated conflict between the primitive impulses of the id and the harshly controlling superego. The second version of ego is what we think of as pride (as in egotism). The latter meaning is how this particular subpersonality is being defined.

The Ego serves your need for social status, which is important for many reasons. While we may associate big egos with people who behave in arrogant, vain, or superior ways, the essential function of the Ego has much more importance than this. Social status has an enormous influence on our security in the world, as it does with many other species. With higher status and rank comes greater respect, recognition, preferential treatment, reproductive opportunities, and other benefits. Your level of status can make the difference between acceptance or rejection, promotion or firing, and approval or disapproval. Your Ego's job is to maximize and preserve your social status.

Establishing status is a highly competitive process. It involves taking measurements of self and others for comparison on a wide range of attributes. Consider the following list of common dimensions with which your Ego may be concerned:

- Intelligence
- Income
- Education
- Physical appearance
- Strength
- Courage
- Popularity
- Vocation
- Material possessions

The Ego is another powerful subpersonality in the psychic family, and its concerns are with maximizing the power that comes with higher status.

The virtue of the Ego is that it helps you "bring home the bacon," by which is meant the entire range of rewards that serve your life. This includes friends, romantic partners, employment opportunities, reputation, popularity, money, sex, marriage and childbearing opportunities, and more. The Ego attempts to make you look as appealing as possible to others, yet it can also be the most unappealing aspect of your personality. The curse side of the Ego is that it can be obnoxiously self-centered. This happens when an Ego places far more emphasis on status than on caring for others. Egotism is often regarded as the opposite of altruism, and there are many religious and social perspectives that demonize this form of selfish pride. But that would be throwing an important baby out with the bathwater. It's entirely possible to have a well-regulated Ego serving the interests of your social reputation while at the same time allowing room for other parts of your personality to remain loving and caring toward others.

The Rebel

The inner Rebel is another powerful and important subpersonality that's a frequently misunderstood underdog in our lives. Rebels have a bad reputation because their nature is to oppose the constraints of authority. Rebels are often oppositional, disruptive, argumentative, uncooperative, and in many other ways a royal pain in the ass. Rebels can be real troublemakers, which is the obvious curse side of the Rebel's nature. And this curse side often obscures the essential virtue of the Rebel's nature.

The true virtue of your Rebel is to acquire and protect your freedom and independence in the world. Whenever you feel subjected to the tyranny and abuses of dominant forces in your life, you may need your Rebel to respond in some way. The term "royal pain" should be a badge of honor for a Rebel, considering how rebels have been the ones to liberate countless people from the oppressive rule of royal monarchies throughout the centuries. The United States was born from a rebellion against the British monarchy, resulting in its Declaration of Independence. George Washington was the country's "rebel in chief" during the Revolutionary War, a founding father and first president of the US, earning the status of the nation's greatest hero. Whether a Rebel is a heroic champion or simply a trouble-making scoundrel all depends on its methods and the consequences of those methods. A well-meaning Rebel can easily become its own worst enemy and undermine its own cause when not tempered by wisdom, perspective, and self-restraint when necessary. On the other hand, inside every artist, inventor, and adventurer is a Rebel who questions the "status quo" and says, "What if…?"

The Romantic

The Romantic is the pursuer of love, intimacy, and ideals. It's another side of the human heart, just as the Nurturer and the Heart are, but the Romantic's pursuits of love are of a different nature. The Romantic often seeks to bond deeply with a partner in ways that combine both emotional and sexual intimacy. But the Romantic may pursue other passions as well in ways that express the heights of love through the arts, humanities, and other personal causes. The virtue of the Romantic is that it orients you toward people and opportunities that hold promise for fulfilling our greatest aspirations for love, partnership, or participation in life's most cherished experiences. The Romantic's curse side is that its intense passions can obscure awareness to risk and harm. Because human passions are rooted in emotion and other senses rather than the analytical mind, they render the heart susceptible to naiveté, deception, seduction, manipulation, and the perils of seeing people and things as we desire to see them rather than as they really are. This is where the notion that "love is blind" comes from. The heights of romantic passion can block out any and all capacity to think reflectively before becoming vulnerable to disappointment. The Romantic can lead us both toward the glories of life and toward the edge of dangerous cliffs at the same time.

The Sexual Self

The Sexual Self is widely recognized as having a *mind of its own* that often is not in agreement with either your Judge or your Heart. Its lustful desires are divorced from both logic and love, as it's governed by an entirely different region of the brain. The Sexual Self is biologically controlled by the hypothalamus, which is located in the limbic region of the brain. It may seem to you as though you are pursuing love or pleasure, but this part of the brain has reproduction as its primary directive. That's not to say that love and lust cannot work together, but rather that they are entirely distinct from one another, and the chances of them becoming integrated in any particular relationship may depend a great deal on how the stars align and how the subpersonalities of each person relate to the subpersonalities of the other.

The Sexual Self serves the virtue of pursuing great pleasure for you as well as motivating you to create new life. You may even be motivated to do great things for the world with the conscious or subconscious realization that doing so will optimize sexual opportunities.

The curse side to the Sexual Self is well understood. This is the part of the self that often doesn't care about other people's feelings or needs. It's supremely selfish by nature and is driven by an urgency that can be so powerful that caution is thrown to the wind and people get hurt in different ways. Not only can this form of blind passion cause harm to others, but it can bring destructive shame, humiliation, condemnation, or even imprisonment on oneself if not carefully managed.

Who's in Charge?

In chapter 10, I explained that the contrasting parts in the subconscious require some form of conductor to serve the role of organizing, managing, integrating, and harmonizing them. If this question was asked in relation to a conventional family, what would you expect the answer to be? Father? Mother? Both? Because each subpersonality in the psyche requires some combination of both control and comfort, the notion that I find more meaningful is one in which the Judge and Nurturer assume the role of co-conductors who operate as a unified team in the regulation of the internal family. The roles of control and comfort are commonly integrated in many families, even in single-parent families. Any individual parent can simultaneously blend the authority necessary for control with the elements of understanding, empathy, and compassion needed for comfort. In fact, both children and adults tend to be most effectively directed when these two elements are combined in some manner. The ratio of control to comfort will not remain the same for dealing with every single subpersonality, as some will require more control than comfort and others just the opposite. Still, the partnership between Judge and Nurturer will create the most effective "voice" needed to address both your core subpersonalities and those that will be introduced as parts of your deeper Shadow (which will be introduced in chapter 14).

Summary

This concludes an introduction to the eight core subpersonalities of the intrapsychic family. The presentation was meant to reveal just how many differences exist between different parts of one's personality, how each of these differences represent both virtues and curses to us, and to assist in recognizing the potential for there to be conflicts between the subpersonalities that exist within us. This is not an exclusive or definitive list of subpersonalities that comprise the subconscious mind, but they are among the universals that we share as complex human beings who need to understand themselves and others more fully if we want to coexist in peace.

CHAPTER 12

Classic Conflicts

Psychologists and other psychotherapists who maintain a psycho-dynamic treatment orientation have long recognized that conflicts between different parts of the subconscious are the cause of much emotional suffering. The miseries of anxiety, depression, guilt, shame, fury, and despair can all exist in the absence of any external conflict and simply be a result of internal conflict. Freudian analytic theory provided the first explanation of this with the example of how the superego conflicted with the id, requiring the ego to mediate between them. Countless varieties of these internal conflicts continue to be recognized by therapists in their offices over a century later.

There is no fixed number of potential conflicts within your psyche, just as there is no fixed number of potential conflicts between you and others. But there are some very common *classic conflicts* that can be easily recognized and understood by most people. These conflicts between value systems exist similarly whether they are found within an individual or between separate individuals. The following examples are some of the most common that can be recognized between and within all people at various points in their lives.

Judge versus Rebel

Judges and Rebels seem to be perpetually in conflict with one another because their contrasting values (control versus freedom) are diametrically opposed. Judges have the responsibility for maintaining control, order, safety, standards, and rules that permit a system of people to interact cohesively. The Judge must have "order in the court," whether that is the court of the family, community, one's country, the globe, or the individual psyche. In contrast, Rebels need to maintain a sense of freedom and independence from excessive domination by Judges and other controlling authorities. It would be a mistake to regard these conflicts as examples of good versus bad or right versus wrong (black-and-white thinking). Each side represents a virtue as well as a threat.

When a Judge is fixed on the goal of establishing control, order, and obedience from its subjects, it can easily lose sight of the values of freedom and autonomy for those subjects. As a consequence, Rebels may become angry enough to begin opposing the Judge's will.

Judges have a range of mechanisms for enforcing control on others. These typically consist of some form of punishment. However, the most potent tool for controlling others or self is the use of shame. Shame is often more threatening and harmful to individuals than many other behavioral punishments because it's capable of damaging or destroying a person's sense of dignity and self-esteem. And, believe it or not, many people shame themselves as a means for regulating their own behavior.

What is important to understand about the conflicts between Judges and Rebels is that excessive force used by either side tends to provoke excessive force from the other side. This is a dynamic that easily turns into a vicious cycle which polarizes Judges and Rebels into rigid enemy positions. This not only destroys one's peace of mind, but it creates the conditions for emotional and behavioral pathology. For instance, if a Judge is overly harsh and controlling, the Rebel may take more advantage of opportunities to escape the Judge's rule through excessive alcohol or drug use (effectively putting the Judge to sleep and liberating the Rebel to go wild). When a Rebel violates the Judge's will through excessive indulgences, the Judge may then come roaring back into power with a greater dose of shame. This form of pendulum swinging can lead to anxiety, guilt, shame, self-loathing, mood swings, and behavior problems.

Although conflicts between Judges and Rebels are as normal as those between parents and teenagers, how these conflicts are managed can make the difference between war and peace. There have been many great rebels who have demonstrated peacefully and effectively (Jesus, Gandhi, Martin Luther, Martin Luther King Jr., Malala Yousafzai). The relationship between Judges and Rebels is a precarious one, and peaceful outcomes will depend on creating a respectful dynamic in the management of these conflicts.

Judge versus Nurturer

The clearest example of the conflict between the values of the Judge and Nurturer is seen in parenting styles. Both types of parents have authentic love and concern for the welfare of their children, yet they will often end up in battles against one another over how to best parent their children. The Judge may say, "Control, discipline, and obedience first," while the Nurturer may say, "Love, comfort, and acceptance first." Both advocate for the virtues of their version of love, but when they oppose one another they often end up doing as much harm to their children as good. The worst case scenario is when the Judge becomes a dictator and the Nurturer becomes a doormat.

Not only is it extremely stressful for children to grow up with parents who are constantly fighting over them, but it can be damaging. Children need to learn that both value systems are necessary, and they also need to learn a model for integrating these values in healthy, peaceful ways. When parents fight, they depict an incompatibility between these values, sowing the seeds of future internal and external conflict in their children's lives. Nowhere is it more important to harmonize the values of Judge and Nurturer than it is in parenting.

Another example of where Judge and Nurturer need to be integrated is in the delivery of healthcare. The western medical model is very scientific, rational, and oriented toward combating disease. But there is more to health and healing than controlling illness in this way. There are also significant psychological dimensions to illness and wellness which are too often neglected by conventional medicine. Sometimes, physical illness causes emotional distress, and oftentimes emotional stress causes physical illness. All too often, patients don't receive the emotionally nurturing care from their doctors that they require for optimal healing. Many doctors and nurses do bring nurturing into their treatments, however this integration of control and comfort is not yet systematic in western training and treatment institutions.

Romantic versus Sexual Self

The conflict between the Romantic and Sexual sides of human nature may be obvious, but deserves explanation. Love and lust serve very different needs. In their purest forms, the Romantic seeks loving intimacy and lasting bonds, while the Sexual Self seeks pleasure and possibly reproduction. The configurations between love and lust manifest themselves differently in males and females, resulting in an abundance of interpersonal conflicts (commonly referred to as "the war of the sexes").

The successful creation of a new generation of offspring requires a complex integration of love and desire. What makes this challenge so complex is that males and females must somehow integrate love and lust within themselves and then integrate love and lust between themselves. These challenges are well explained by the author John Gray in his books, <u>Men Are From Mars/Women Are From Venus</u> (1992), and <u>Mars and Venus in the Bedroom</u> (2009).

Further complicating the integration of love and lust is the tendency for other subpersonalities to take sides in the conflict between them. The Judge, Nurturer, and Heart may all favor the values of the Romantic, while the Rebel and Ego may side with the Sexual Self. Such chaos and division explain a lot about why adolescence is such a turbulent stage of human development, because this is precisely the age during which the Romantic, Sexual Self, Ego, and Rebel are coming into existence, disrupting the equilibrium of the Heart and creating a whole new world of conflict for the Judge to somehow manage.

Judge, Ego and Warrior versus Heart and Nurturer

Another version of conflicting alliances in the subconscious is when the Judge, Ego, and Warrior join forces in opposition to the Heart and Nurturer. On a very primitive level, this is essentially a division between power and vulnerability or strength and weakness. In some ways it also reflects a division between masculine and feminine natures. For reasons having to do with both biology and socialization, boys often develop their competitive, controlling, and domineering powers preparing them for the roles of provider and protector, while girls develop more heart-centered relationship skills that prepare them to be nurturing wives and mothers, nurses and teachers. But there is nothing to dictate that these value systems must be divided along gender lines or prevent both genders from integrating all of these values. When these contrasting value systems are viewed competitively, an unfortunate antagonism interferes with them being integrated and balanced, both within individuals and between them.

It's important that our boys and men learn to embrace their emotionally sensitive Hearts and their Nurturing aptitudes. Likewise, it's imperative that our girls and women embrace their Judge, Warrior, and Ego natures. And it's imperative that everyone learns to integrate these contrasting elements within the psyche and with their love partners, regardless of gender.

Judge versus Sexual Self

The conflicts between the Judge and the Sexual Self take us right back to Freud's observations about the conflictual relationship between the superego and the id. The impersonal and selfish nature of unrestrained lust presents a threat to a civil society, and thus all cultures have had to evolve behavioral standards to regulate the expression of sexuality. The use of social shame may be the most universal means for accomplishing this. Individual Judges (consciences) learn early in life to be distrustful of unbridled lust in others and within themselves, not only to prevent sexual victimization, but to avoid public shame, vilification, humiliation, and imprisonment.

While it's true that shame is a highly effective mechanism for controlling the "devil" within us, it can also cause excessive harm when misused. If one's natural sexuality becomes associated with shame, humiliation, embarrassment, fear, and other consequences of harsh judgment, this can impair a healthy integration of sexuality with the Heart and in relationships with love partners. Sexuality needs to be *tamed*, but not *demonized*, in order to be expressed in healthy ways.

Heart versus Sexual Self

Both the Heart and the Sexual Self fuel powerful attractions to other people, though for sharply contrasting reasons. The Heart is attracted to people who may provide elements conducive to emotional intimacy, nurturance, trust, safety, comfort, and bonding, while the Sexual Self is attracted to those who arouse physical desire and pleasure. These contrasting attractions generate tensions within and between individuals. Such tensions emerge during adolescence in the transition from being Heart-centered children into sexual beings, creating disruptions to one's sense of self and identity. The resulting confusions impact how teenagers feel about themselves and how they behave toward others to whom they're attracted. Some will embrace lustful feelings eagerly, while others may feel ashamed and disgusted by them. Many will have a combination of both reactions, excitement and aversion, to their developing sexuality. Teenagers are given no instruction manual to help them understand or create a new order out of this sudden disorder. The Heart and Sexual Self may compete with one another indefinitely, unless or until a relationship with another inspires them to facilitate their alignment.

The chaotic tensions between the Heart and Sexual Self may begin in adolescence, but they are by no means resolved in the transition from adolescence to adulthood. And, for many they are never resolved. The opposing values of love and lust may churn out confusion, guilt, shame, embarrassment, humiliation, and despair indefinitely, often representing the greatest obstacle to peace over the course of one's lifespan. Judge and Nurturer may side with the Heart, the Rebel and Ego may support the Sexual Self, but so long as there are divides between their camps, peace will be compromised, both within and between people. For many, healing the divide between the Heart and Sexual Self will be the most important investment necessary for creating a more peaceful life.

Summary

The classic conflicts between subpersonalities described in this chapter are not the only ones that can disturb life's inner and outer peace. They have been highlighted both because they are universal conflicts and because they offer clear illustrations of the conflicts naturally occurring within and between people on a regular basis. Each depicts a set of contrasting values that will hurt us when they collide with one another, and they will serve us best when they can be integrated and harmonized. They reflect the multiplicity of human nature and the necessity of managing conflicts between the subpersonalities that exist within every individual as a stepping stone toward managing conflict with others who embody these same differences. Each of these classic conflicts requires the assistance of control (Judge) and comfort (Nurturer) to ensure the best outcomes. And this is why the foundation of healing and peace, the management of all conflicts, relies upon your Judge and Nurturer becoming models of collaboration. Together, they must recognize the common identity shared by the subpersonalities and use this awareness as the key for living by the Golden Rule. We must learn to love others as we love ourselves, because others are in fact a part of ourselves.

CHAPTER 13

The Shadow of Shame

There is more to the subconscious mind than the eight core sub-personalities introduced in chapter 11. Carl Gustav Jung, one of Freud's contemporaries and another founding father of psychoanalytic theory, introduced the term *shadow* to refer to a darker territory of the subconscious where the most undesirable elements of human consciousness get buried. The shadow is less accessible to conscious awareness than the core subpersonalities, and for good reason. This is a hiding place for feelings, impulses, urges, thoughts, desires, and memories that we do not want others or ourselves to be aware of. Hiding undesirable elements in the shadow is a defense mechanism that protects the conscious mind from becoming overwhelmed by guilt, shame, embarrassment, humiliation, and despair. It's a form of denial that works quite well, up to a point. Hiding this material from your awareness doesn't mean that it won't affect you, only that it won't threaten to ruin you. This shadow content will still disturb your peace over time, doing so by generating distressing psychological and physical symptoms that you may not recognize as emanating from this repository of shame. It may express itself in your nightmares or come out under the influence of alcohol or drugs. The shadow is the proverbial rug under which we sweep our collective dirt, and shame is the most powerful broom used to sweep it there.

The fullest healing and peace of mind requires us to address our shadow material. In some ways it's as though our inner demons will continue to haunt us unless or until we bring to them the elements of healing and peace. One way to think of the inhabitants of the shadow is like prisoners who have been locked away without being provided with any rehabilitation or hope for release. Under such conditions these prisoners will only grow more desperate and dangerous, looking for any weak moment to break out and wreak havoc on the civilized world that has banished them. The walls that imprison the inhabitants of the shadow are made of shame, and although shame is an extremely powerful mechanism of control and suppression, its toxic nature will contaminate other areas of the psyche and impose limits on the heights of peace we are able to reach.

Imagine that your destination of healing and peace lies at the top of a distant mountain, and lying between you and that mountain top is the jungle of the shadow. It's sort of like Dorothy and her companions being told they must bring back the broomstick of the Wicked Witch of the West if they wish to reclaim their heart, mind, courage, and a way home. But the journey through the shadow jungle is neither a witch hunt nor any other form of conquering mission. In order to reach your destination you must bring the skills of peacemaking and healing to the demons you have cast there to be forgotten.

One can be forgiven for not wanting to embark on such a journey because accessing this deeper region of the psyche entails real risk. In fact, it's strongly advised to not undertake this process without the professional support of a well-trained psychologist, psychotherapist, or spiritual guide. Those who do this best are those who have undergone this journey themselves. Additionally, this is a stage of healing that should not be undertaken without first establishing a sound foundation of psychological stability. That structure begins with the five pillars of healing and peace being securely in place and having an unbreakable alliance between your Judge and Nurturer. It will also be necessary to have already utilized that alliance to develop a cohesive integration between the eight core subpersonalities of your mind. This is important because the intensity of your shadow material threatens to destabilize divisions between your subpersonalities, leaving you with less peace of mind than before you started this leg of the journey.

The popular Pixar movie, <u>How to Train Your Dragon,</u> provides another comforting metaphor for how terrifying beasts can be tamed and trained to become safe allies in life. Instead of demonizing what we naturally find dangerous, learning how to understand and relate to it using Golden Rule principles is the secret for this transformation. Instead of maintaining maximum divisions between ourselves and those we distrust by maintaining walls of shame, we must learn how to replace shame with mechanisms of control that are not damaging to those we fear. Remember, those we fear share a common identity with us, and so we only harm ourselves when we harm others with shame.

The opposites within us are completely natural. Integrating these opposites creates a foundation of strength, harmony, and peace. The motto for the seal of the United States, "E Pluribus Unum," embodies two meanings – "The one is made up of all things, and all things issue from the one." The shadow is simply one more domain for this truth to be realized. In the next chapter, introductions will be made to some of the universal inhabitants of the shadow.

CHAPTER 14

Shady Characters

Every human mind possesses remnants of primitive instincts (impulses, desires, drives, and urges) that offer potential survival value to us. When we are fortunate enough to have all our basic needs for survival met, these instincts are not only less critical to rely on, but they often become maladaptive in a rule-governed society, and therefore they need to be reined in. But if we were to live under conditions where the basic resources for survival were extremely scarce, then these instincts would once again become critical assets. Imagine living in a world without any rule of law other than "survival of the fittest," where food and fuel supplies were inadequate for the population, there was no social order or system of justice, and everyone lived in fear and desperation. Under these circumstances your values would need to change dramatically for you and your loved ones to survive. Doing so might depend on instincts for dishonesty, manipulation, aggression, stealing, and whatever else would be necessary to simply avoid death. The codes for such conduct have been written into your

DNA because they were required in the prehistoric stages of human evolution. In the modern age they are far less essential for survival, but they remain part of your nature, needing to be controlled, and possessing the potential for disturbing your peace if you don't understand how to manage them properly.

This chapter introduces a set of 10 names and explanations for these darker archetypes of the human subconscious. There is no consensus for how many of these subpersonalities exist or how they are best defined. However they are being presented in a manner intended to make them more recognizable and relatable to most readers. There are several things that each of these subpersonalities have in common. They can all jeopardize healing and peace by creating conditions for excessive punishment, anxiety, guilt and shame, and they must all be carefully retrained. At the same time, if they are over-regulated by judgment, guilt, and shame, they may become the source of psychic wounds that will require healing in order to restore greater peace of mind. Therefore, any of these subpersonalities will require the well-integrated and balanced influences of a Judge/Nurturer partnership to manage and care for them.

The Liar

Everybody lies, of course, though not all lies are equally harmful. There are white lies that may cause no harm or may even prevent harm. There are lies that benefit oneself at the expense of others, and lies that protect oneself from others. Lies that serve ourselves at the expense of others are those for which we are meant to feel guilty. We lie mostly when we feel threatened or vulnerable in some way, and so lying under these circumstances may be a necessary choice to minimize danger.

Regardless of how justifiable we consider our lies to be, they nonetheless create risks for us. If we are caught lying, we face the prospects of punishment and damage to trust and reputation, causing a loss of social status. Even when lies go undetected, we may live with ongoing anxiety, guilt, or shame for having told them, because the Judge keeps track of our dishonesties.

The Thief

Your inner Thief is another shady character capable of violating the rules of society. The Thief takes what does not belong to her or him for any number of reasons. Like the motivations of the other shady characters, there is a kernel of adaptive value in thievery. Any parent of starving children will commit theft in order to survive because survival trumps honesty for all of us. But survival isn't the only motivation that underlies thievery. The Thief may be a rebel and/or avenger seeking to right imbalances in your system of justice (think Robin Hood). Sometimes, thieves are fueled by greed or the thrill of the cat and mouse game. Whether a Thief's motives are for survival, greed, or gamesmanship, it will disturb your peace if it is either under-regulated or overly castigated by guilt and shame. Your Judge and Nurturer will need to work together to find the appropriate way to address your Thief within the context of its transgressions.

The Greed Monster

The Greed Monster represents your instinct for more – more money, power, attention, and possessions. It's an adaptive instinct under circumstances of deprivation. Sometimes, greed has nothing to do with the anxieties of deprivation, but more to do with the competitive nature of the Ego to feel superior to others by acquiring more than they have. Greed is most heavily scorned when an individual's pursuit of resources conflicts with a fair distribution of those resources among the larger group, especially when an individual takes far more resources than are actually necessary for his or her survival. While the self-serving instinct to gather more and more resources needs to be regulated, it must be done so with the understanding that this instinct has made its contributions to your survival over the millennia.

The Bully

Nobody likes bullies, except perhaps their allies. Bullies abuse their power by taking power away from others through acts of domination. Not all forms of domination are bullying (parents must exert dominant control over their children), but domination for the purpose of taking power away from others in order to maximize one's own power is abusive, hostile, and often destructive. Yet even bullying has it adaptive survival value. Bullying is most often motivated by desperate insecurities regarding an inadequacy of one's own power. In order to compensate for perceptions of inferiority, bullies need to create an image of superiority to themselves and others. And one of the most effective ways to create an image of superiority is by making others feel inferior.

Bullies actually need a lot of help. While the abusive behavior of the Bully needs to be restrained, the deep-seated vulnerabilities of inferiority and inadequacy must also be addressed compassionately. Once again, this calls for a carefully unified approach by the wise Judge/Nurturer partnership.

The Destroyer

Anyone familiar with the nature of 10-year-old boys will recognize how the instinct to be destructive lives in even the sweetest among us. The instinct to destroy has a number of different values. One of the most basic of these is the need to feel powerful. Boys are typically more concerned with becoming powerful than girls are, in part because boys are socialized to acquire and display power, aggressiveness, courage, and the ability to protect self and others from other destructive powers. It's a natural response to the fear of being destroyed that we seek the power to be destroyers ourselves. A related motive of the Destroyer is the desire to eliminate whatever may be a cause for suffering. Anything we may interpret as an enemy the Destroyer may seek to vanquish. This instinct can also apply to other parts of oneself. When there are perceptions that a part or parts within are suffering (ie. the sensitive Heart, the insatiable Ego, the tyrannical Judge, the lustful Sexual Self, etc), the Destroyer may turn its aggression toward those parts it holds responsible for the internal distress.

Like all other subpersonalities, the Destroyer has both adaptive value and risky liabilities and it's important not to throw its baby out with the bathwater. The Destroyer needs to be restrained from going too far, yet the need for the cultivation of appropriate power needs to be preserved, and anxieties about being powerless need to be comforted.

The Avenger

The Avenger is commonly fueled by righteous rage, and its purpose is to balance the scales of justice through any means necessary. Whenever there is a perception (or misperception) of injustice resulting in harm to self or loved ones, your Avenger may go on the warpath. Avengers can be true heroes serving the cause of justice, but they may also become villains themselves if not properly restrained. There are reasons that civil societies have judicial systems that protect the rights of the accused, otherwise Avengers might go overboard, persecuting witches, heretics, rebels, or others who remind them of past tormentors. When Avengers are blinded by rage, they may wrongfully punish undeserving people in ways that are out of proportion to their transgressions. The excesses of vengeance can backfire when they perpetuate ever greater injustices, and thus these powerful urges are in need of both restraint and comforting.

The Jealous

There is nothing pleasant about the experience of jealousy for those who experience it or those who are the subject of it. Jealousy is a bitterness associated with others having something that we desperately feel we need and deserve. It can inspire animosity toward others and the impulse to act in hostile ways ("If I can't have what I want, then you don't deserve it either"). Those who suffer from jealousy often suffer from deeper feelings of inadequacy, inferiority, and deprivations in their Hearts. It's not enough to regulate any hostile impulse inspired by jealousy, but we must also provide nurturing comfort to those places that feel hurt when it appears that others are getting what is so desired for oneself.

The Hedonist

Your inner Hedonist is that part of your nature that is simply preoccupied with pleasure and self-satisfaction in all its forms. There is nothing wrong with the enjoyment of pleasure within limits, although the pure hedonist knows no bounds. Unchecked, it can crave unhealthy amounts or types of pleasure. As the saying goes, too much of a good thing isn't good. The Hedonist can get out of control with its cravings for a number of reasons. For instance, when the Heart has become closed as a consequence of excessive suffering or deprivations, this void may give rise to a compensating appetite for pleasure in order to stave off feelings of despair. The natural desire for pleasure can easily get out of balance when there is a lack of adequate limits placed on pleasure, leading to addictive cravings. All sources of pleasure— sexuality, sweets, intoxication, and entertainment, can be worthwhile in the proper measure and harmful when taken to extremes. Pleasure can be a great way to reward ourselves for doing important things that are inherently unpleasant. So don't throw this baby out with the bathwater either, but instead learn to understand, appreciate, and indulge your inner Hedonist while at the same time maintaining adequate levels of control over its thirst for excess.

The Hater

Everyone has the capacity to feel hatred, though people differ widely in the sources of their hatred and the targets toward which they direct their hatred. Hatred is more intense than anger, powerful enough to cause harm to both the hated and the hater. The function of hatred is to condemn and reject those things or people that we consider unacceptable. In this regard there is a potential survival value to hatred, wanting those people or things that are threatening to oneself to no longer be a part of one's life. However, like judgment, hatred often has a boomerang effect, causing those who hate too often to become hated themselves. Hatred is divisive, and divisions are often destabilizing.

In the extreme, hatred leads to violence and war, both the complete antithesis of healing and peace. The outward expression of hatred needs to be curtailed for the sake of interpersonal peace, and the inward experience of hatred needs to be soothed in order to prevent this toxic emotion from completely destroying the potential for inner healing and peace.

The challenge of soothing hatred can be a great one because the true cause of hatred is not always clear based upon to whom or at what the hatred is being directed. Even the person consumed by hatred may not understand the original source of it. Discovering this requires an exploration of the deepest levels of emotional agony, which often consist of extreme fear and sadness. These vulnerabilities may be difficult to access because the power of hatred effectively obscures them, and many people prefer the strength of hatred to the comparative feeling of weakness that lies beneath it. Hatred arises from deep wounds that are heavily guarded and therefore not easily uncovered for the purpose of healing them. But this is the only way for hatred to truly be released. To access these wounds, the hatred must be acknowledged with respect and understanding first, rather than being judged or demonized. Only then will this guardian of pain consider exposing the deeper origins of the hate that is rooted in agony. When that happens, the Nurturer will need to respond with tremendous compassion to begin the healing process.

The Victim

Everyone suffers from victimization at some point in their lives. Whether victimization results in forming a part of your identity depends on the nature, degree, and duration of victimization, as well as how you respond to the experience. It's seldom the case that anyone wants to be regarded as a victim, although there are certain benefits to it that are deserved. Victims require our sympathy, concern, and support, and we must extend certain allowances to victims when they become disabled by their hardships. On the other hand, victims are sometimes scorned or even blamed for their victim status. How people respond to a soldier suffering from PTSD may differ greatly from how they respond to an intoxicated coed who is sexually assaulted at a fraternity party. There's a lot at stake in the "victim game," namely, who is going to bear the brunt of the blame and shame. All too often innocent victims are vilified by those who wish to protect powerful abusers from the consequences of their offenses, and the most effective way to do this is often to find a way to blame the victim. This is why the vast majority of victims of sexual abuse don't risk reporting their assaults.

Whichever way one ends up being victimized, whether this results in assuming a Victim identity depends a lot on whether this identity is embraced or denied. There are advantages and disadvantages to both choices. Becoming overly attached to a Victim identity may interfere with a return to a non-Victim sense of self. Denying a Victim status may result in living with unreasonable expectations and demands being imposed upon a person whose capabilities are legitimately diminished. There are tremendous vulnerabilities associated with being a Victim, and this part of one's identity therefore requires a great deal of sensitivity and care. The Victim needs compassion, understanding, empathy, support, and release from unreasonable expectations in order to allow for the possibility of recovering. At the same time, Victims may need encouragement to reclaim their lost powers and strive toward assuming an identity that is not overly limited by the trappings of the Victim role. Battered women's shelters are dedicated to providing this kind of support, safety, and encouragement. The teamwork of the Judge and Nurturer will be of vital importance for navigating this delicate balance of survival and recovery.

PART III

The Process of Healing
and Creating Peace

CHAPTER 15

The Destruction and Restoration of Wholeness

Wholeness is much easier to destroy than it is to create or restore. The key to understanding how to restore wholeness lies in an understanding of how it's destroyed in the first place.

Peace is an experience characterized by wholeness and harmony – much like an orchestra of unified musicians playing their individual parts collaboratively to create music that none could create on their own or without a skilled conductor. To destroy the harmony of this music, all that's necessary is to create hostile divisions within the orchestra, turning individuals or sections against one another to the extent that they would be unable to agree on what music to play, how it would be played, or who would conduct their performance. And the most simple and powerful way to destroy unity would be to introduce judgment and shame into the orchestra. If the conductor were to abuse the musicians with judgment or shame, it would diminish the orchestra's ability and/or willingness to create beautiful music together. If the string section used these abuses against the wind section or the percussionists, the same thing would happen.

Judgment and shame are destructive because they are divisive. When people or groups are sharply divided as a result of judgment and shame, not only are they less capable of working together, but the chances increase that they will work *against* each other. The consequences of judgment and shame are so threatening that they cause their own version of fight or flight in response. With either response there can be no wholeness or harmony.

The restoration of wholeness and harmony is much more difficult than its destruction, just as a city is harder to rebuild than it is to bomb into ruins. Recovery and restoration take longer not only because it takes time to rebuild a damaged city, but because it takes even more time to repair the relationship with the enemy that dropped the bombs in the first place. In truth, time alone does not heal all wounds. And complete healing of divisions cannot be done in isolation. A destroyed city or country may be able to rebuild itself in time, but the damage to the relationship with its conquering enemy would require the assistance of the enemy to heal it.

Put more simply, wholeness is destroyed when judgment creates division, conflict, and enmity. Restoring wholeness requires a repair of internal damage plus repair of damaged relationships. For the mind, the internal repair that's necessary includes the cleansing of shame, fear, and hatred that was caused by the assaults of judgment and shame. Relationship repairs require a restoration of trust through the efforts of understanding, release of judgment, forging new agreements, and rebuilding collaborative alliances. This is true for the relationships between all *others*, be they separate countries, individuals, or subpersonalities within an individual.

The following chapters explain the dynamics of judgment and shame more completely as they apply to the individual psyche. It's important to understand these general dynamics before learning about the stages of healing and restoring wholeness that will be introduced in part 4.

CHAPTER 16

The Dangers of Judgment

Judgment, and the guilt and shame that it causes, lies at the heart of many of our emotional and relationship troubles. One of the greatest secrets to creating wholeness of mind and peaceful relationships is learning how to stop being judgmental. Here's why.

We all judge, and there is a place for judgment that's appropriate, useful, and necessary in order for us to regulate behavior and coexist in a civilized society. But a distinction needs to be made between two forms of judgment—one that is helpful and another that is harmful. The helpful version of judgment serves the function of *assessment*. Parents need to assess the behavior of their children in order to improve it. Teachers need to assess the thinking of their students in order to develop it. Employers need to assess the work of their employees in order to advance it. People must learn to assess themselves in order to guide their own functioning and growth. These are judgments about how we think and behave that are intended to help us improve ourselves. Judgments for the purposes of assessing and guiding thought and behavior are helpful when done properly.

Judgments that are harmful to wholeness and health are those that target an individual's identity in ways that disempower them. When judgments go beyond assessing thought and behavior to the level of *identity*, such judgments are deeply offensive. They may not only cause hurt, but may do lasting harm. Personal judgments do not merely assess—they condemn.

Condemning judgments are the primary cause of toxic shame. These judgments strike directly at the core of who we are as people, impacting experiences of self-worth and identity.

Most people are not clear in their understanding of the difference between assessing judgments and condemning judgments, especially children. When parents are merely trying to reprimand a child's inappropriate behavior, that child might misinterpret the judgment to mean that s/he is a bad child. Therefore it's important that those making judgments are clear about the difference and careful in how they convey their judgments. Likewise, it's equally important that receivers of judgment are clear about the difference and don't misinterpret assessment as condemnation.

Judgment can be damaging to others either when it's expressed carelessly or when it's intentionally used as a weapon. Either way it's wise to be careful in the expression of judgment because *judgment has a boomerang effect.* Whenever you target someone with a judgment there are two ways that it may come back to hurt you. The most common example of this is, "What goes around, comes around." People have tit-for-tat instincts, and so those who judge others in condemning ways set themselves up for being condemned by others as well.

There is a second way that judgments can boomerang back. When you condemn the identity of another person you are unwittingly condemning a part of yourself. The characteristic that you may be condemning in another person will likely be a characteristic that also exists within the shadow of your own subconscious. Because of this, the more forceful you are in your judgments of others, the more difficult it will be to create a state of peaceful wholeness within yourself.

The Golden Rule tells us to "Love others as you would have them love you," not "Judge others as you would have them judge you." The Bible exhorts believers to "Judge not, lest you be judged." Other religious traditions share this perspective, though there is confusion in many traditions resulting from the lack of clarity about assessing and condemning judgments. Regard your condemning judgments as boomerangs that cause damage to those they are thrown at, as well as to those who throw them.

CHAPTER 17

Shame: Purge or Project

We all embody various forms and degrees of shame within our hearts and minds. Shame is one of the most powerful emotional tools there is for controlling ourselves and others. It serves the functions of preventing that which should be prevented and motivating us to do what needs to be done. It's the force behind our *shoulds and shouldn'ts.* There are forms of shame that are valuable to us, such as the shame that prevents us from abusing those with less power than ourselves. But there is also toxic shame that causes much more harm than good. Toxic shame is like putting rat poison in a baby's nursery to protect it from rats, but which poisons the baby along with the rats. Shame may serve us well up to a point, but its overuse contributes to psychopathology.

Toxic shame needs to be purged from your psyche if you hope for deep and abiding peace within yourself and with others. Shame imparts the stigma of "bad/wrong" in the most forceful way possible. Guilt also carries the "bad/wrong" message, although guilt targets a person's *behavior,* whereas shame targets a person's *identity.* There's a huge difference between feeling guilty for *what one has done* versus feeling ashamed for *who one is*. You cannot create wholeness and peace within yourself if you harbor the belief that who you are is "bad or wrong."

As previously explained, one way to protect yourself from the destructive influence of toxic shame is to bury your bad/wrong parts in the shadow region of your mind. But this form of protection is temporary and superficial at best, because what you blind yourself to internally, you will eventually project onto others.

Projection is the psychological defense mechanism of misperceiving something that exists *inside* of oneself as only existing on the *outside* of oneself. Denial and projection typically work hand-in-hand as defense mechanisms against shame. The price for this protection is that it's destructive to those upon whom we project our shame and to our relationships with those scapegoats. This is also a rigidly held form of self-deception that prevents people from changing and growing. Many alcoholics and drug addicts in recovery programs have learned the hard way that *denial is the disease*, meaning that you can't change what you can't accept responsibility for. When you can face and own the nature of your weaknesses, that is where you will find the greatest hope for finding new strengths.

But who wouldn't rather be the shamer of others than to feel vulnerable to being shamed by others? Instinctively we know that it's safer to be the shamer than to be the shamed. Yet this is not a true path to safety or peace. Shame is hurtful and divisive to individuals and to their relationships with others. Those we shame will fear us and possibly even hate us, be they our loved ones or those with whom we are in conflict. Shame may serve to provide some measure of control when it's needed, but such control comes at the expense of peace, trust, integration, and collaboration. When precious lives are involved, sometimes it's better to use mouse traps than rat poison to protect them from harm.

The lesson here is this: true peace does not result from denying the shame you carry in the shadows of your minds and projecting it onto others. True peace requires you to cleanse the toxic residues of shame from your shadow and then heal the damage caused by it.

CHAPTER 18

Integrating the Sacred and the Profane

Perhaps the most polar opposite extremes of human nature are those of the sacred and the profane that dwell within us all. Rather than considering them as subpersonalities, they might generally be thought of as *territories* of the mind, with the profane residing in the darkness of your shadow and the sacred residing in the light of your spirituality or humane conscience. The cartoon version of this difference is that of an angel on one shoulder and the devil on the other, each making their best arguments to influence our choices.

When the sacred and profane sides of human nature are too polarized, individuals may experience what they perceive as some form of holy war. Holy wars are dangerous experiences. A holy war is any determination to destroy what might be branded as "evil" from a black-and-white perspective of righteous moral certainty. Such wars can take place between religions or between a religion and a secular group. But a holy war can take place within an individual's mind as well. Internal holy wars occur between the sacred and profane sides of one's identity. When a person's psyche is set on fire with the zeal to destroy the threat of evil, this creates a form of psychopathology. This "kill or be killed" mentality is pathological because it's destructive to others and self at the same time. People afflicted by this psychopathology can never experience true wholeness or peace.

The integration of the sacred and profane sides of human nature is important to understand properly. This integration certainly doesn't mean that they cancel one another out or take turns swinging back and forth like a pendulum. So, how are they to be balanced and integrated?

There are several versions of a Native American Indian legend that captures the nature of the struggle between the sacred and profane sides of human nature. The Cherokee version of this legend goes as follows:

> An old Cherokee is teaching his grandson about life. "A fight is going on inside me," he said to the boy.
>
> "It's a terrible fight and it's between two wolves. One is evil—he is anger, envy, sorrow, regret, greed, arrogance, self-pity, resentment, inferiority, lies, false pride, superiority, and ego." He continued, "The other is good—he is joy, peace, love, hope, serenity, humility, kindness, benevolence, empathy, generosity, truth, compassion, and faith. The same fight is going on inside you—and inside every other person, too."
>
> The grandson thought about it for a minute and then asked his grandfather, "Which wolf will win?"
>
> The old Cherokee simply replied, "The one you feed."

It's true that the side of our nature that we feed with the most attention will likely become the side that has the greatest influence over our thoughts, feelings, and behaviors. However, it's important to understand that simply neglecting to pay attention to the profane wolves in your shadow will neither starve them out of existence nor render them harmless, because a starving wolf can become desperate and ravenously out of control to fight for its survival. Therefore, the regulation of your different wolves requires *feeding, taming, and training* them, along with the strategic use of *fences* to prevent your more dangerous wolves from encroaching into peaceful territories.

The wise wolf-keeper will provide understanding, respect, and caring attention to all wolves according to their needs and natures. By doing so, the sacred and profane wolf packs can find ways of coexisting in relative peace, as both packs will share a respect for the wise keeper's will. Just as the pagan roots of Halloween involved rituals designed to make peace with the demons of the spirit world, so too, the wise wolf-keeper learns to maintain peaceful influence over the two packs.

Human tames wolf, wolf serves human

Humans and wolves have historically been competitors and threats to one another. However, somewhere in time humans and wolves recognized value in establishing collaborative relationships with one another which eventually resulted in wolves becoming the first non-human species to become domesticated. As a result, both species have benefitted immeasurably.

Today's dogs, the domesticated descendants of wolves, serve humans in ways that go well beyond the affectionate companionship they provide. They serve survival needs such as assistance with hunting and protection. They may even pull sleds or fetch slippers. They can track runaway fugitives or locate survivors buried in rubble. They can guide the blind and provide therapeutic support for the disabled. They assist law enforcement by sniffing out drugs, explosives, or tackling violent offenders. Some can even detect the presence of illness or pre-seizure activity in the ill.

If you can fathom the difference resulting from converting the relationship between humans and wolves from a competitive rivalry for survival into a mutually beneficial collaboration, this should provide you with a way to consider the value of taming and integrating your shadow subpersonalities into your identity. Just as we have with wolves, by understanding their nature and their needs, respecting their powers, earning their trust, feeding and petting them, bringing these same skills to your relationship with your shadow subpersonalities will serve you in similar ways.

The story of the relationship between humans and wolves illustrates how evil is often perceived in the eyes of the beholder, and how mortal enmity can be transformed into holy alliances with the right perspective and care. Demonizing and waging war on others who threaten us is never a path to peace. This is the wisdom necessary for the journey into the shadow for the sake of healing and transforming the relationship between the sacred and profane sides of your own nature.

PART IV

Programming Peace Into the Subconscious

CHAPTER 19

From Understanding to Realization

As the saying goes, "You can lead a horse to water, but you can't make it drink." This notion has many applications, including finding peace and healing emotional wounds. Being a psychotherapist is a humbling experience because all the training and experience of a lifetime does not endow a therapist with the ability to bring peace and healing to the clients with whom s/he works. There are many different reasons why horses won't drink the water that they are led to, but there's only one reason that I'm going to focus on in this brief chapter, and it has to do with the difference between understanding and realization.

In my work and in this writing, I have endeavored to do my best to teach the principles of creating peace and healing. But even if I have done this well enough for clients and readers to understand these principles, that is not sufficient for peace and healing to occur, because there is an enormous divide between *understanding* something and having it become *realized*. The difference between understanding and realization is akin to reading a book about the joys of sex versus actually having sex. To have the experience of something requires more than simply understanding it with the rational mind. When it comes to realizing peace and healing, a better analogy would be if you were to put two unacquainted people in a room together and have them read a book about friendship. Assuming the book was written well enough that both readers fully grasped the nature and process of how to become friends, this would still not result in the two automatically becoming friends with each other. For that to happen, they would have to take the additional step of *applying* their understanding by interacting with one another using the skills they learned in the book. Only when their understanding is put into experience through personal interaction would there be any possibility of making a friendship real.

Creating peace of mind and healing emotional wounds both require the creation of new experiences that will have you interacting with each of your subpersonalities and preparing them to interact with one another. You will need to have dialogues with your Heart, Judge, Nurturer, Warrior, Rebel, Ego, Romantic, and Sexual Self, *and* have them begin transformative dialogues with one another. Applying the five pillars of healing and peace to these dialogues will create a foundation for a more peaceful mind. Once that is established, more peace can be pursued by going on a healing journey to the subpersonalities in the shadow jungle of your mind. All of this means being prepared to have a lot of dialogues, and that will take a lot more time than necessary to simply read and understand this book. For readers appreciating the computer metaphor, upgrading the OS to improve the performance of your computer requires more than simply downloading it or receiving it in the mail — it will need to be installed on the computer before it will make any difference.

What you are preparing to do is to change your mind. Doing so begins with acquiring new understandings with your conscious mind, then delivering and installing these understandings to your subconscious mind. This delivery and installation process is achieved through relational experiences, and these relational experiences consists of a series of dialogues. That is how you change your mind. That is how you install a new program that will eventually work automatically for you, because you will be encoding it into your subconscious. The real benefits of what you've been learning up to this point will only be realized once you invest the time to have these dialogues with your subpersonalities. That is how you will proceed from understanding to realization.

Here's how this part of the book will unfold. Chapter 21 will introduce you to the Capacchione method for dialoguing with your subconscious mind. Chapter 22 will offer a recipe for peace talks to use in your dialogues with your subpersonalities. This same recipe will also serve your need to have more peaceful dialogues with others in your life. Chapter 23 will provide exercises to get you started with these dialogues.

The exercises in chapter 23 are designed only to foster greater peace, integration, and healing in the relationships among your eight core subpersonalities. For healing to take place among the wounded subpersonalities of your shadow, more work will need to be done either independently or ideally with the assistance of a skilled therapist. There are two reasons for this recommendation. First, it's not advisable to enter into deeper levels of emotional pain and division unless or until there is a solid foundation established between the eight core subpersonalities first. Second, the shadow territory is more intense, complex, and fragile, and therefore is risky to pursue without the safety net and guidance of a skilled therapist. That said, if you are someone who is able to practice the skills in this book successfully enough to create peace and healing among the eight core subpersonalities on your own, you might be able to bring your skills into the shadow territory to effect greater peace and healing there. No one should proceed beyond the limits of their safety, stability, and capacity to function responsibly in their lives.

The scope of these introductory exercises will be limited even within the context of creating greater peace and healing among your eight core subpersonalities. The goal of this book is only to teach the principles and the techniques for applying them rather than going the distance to complete self-healing. If you can get your horse to drink from these waters and trust them, then it will be up to you how far to continue on your own quest for deeper peace and healing. Many will be able to go far on their own, while others will benefit from continuing their efforts with a skilled guide.

CHAPTER 20

The Socratic Method

The ancient Greek philosopher, Socrates (469-399 BC), is credited with developing one of the most widely used methods for discovering "truth" through the use of dialogue. This dialectical process (known as the Socratic method) involves two parties engaging in an exchange of questions and answers designed to test the validity of a theory or some notion of truth. What makes the Socratic method different from argumentative debate is that the exchange is a *collaborative* one in which the shared goal of the two parties is to uncover truth rather than for one party to defeat the other in a competition over truth. The Socratic method implies working together for answers rather than working against one another, and this dynamic of collaboration provides added value in the search for truth. This is quite different than courtroom contests that often have very little to do with forming a consensus about truth, and instead is a battle to determine whose version of the truth will win, regardless of the accuracy of that version.

The Socratic method has been adopted by several schools of psychotherapy, most notably cognitive therapy, as a tool for reprogramming the mind. Because the method involves a dialogue between contrasting points of view, it is inherently *reflective* in nature, helping to convert black-and-white beliefs into more adaptive rainbow perspectives.

The easiest way to learn and practice the Socratic method for the purpose of examining and adjusting your mind's OS is to find a trained therapist to do this with, however it's also entirely possible for some people to do so independently. Whether the Socratic method is utilized in therapy or independently, there are specific elements that make this method more effective than an ordinary dialogue, debate, or argument. Chapter 25 will provide an explanation for how to make these dialogues as safe and effective as possible by applying the five pillars of healing and peace. These are the same elements that make therapeutic dialogues most effective. Therefore you will be learning to communicate like a good therapist, and this will ultimately prepare you for becoming your own therapist. Not only that, but these communication skills will make you a more effective spouse, parent, friend, or coworker, because these methods are not only for healing, but also for managing conflicts, solving problems, and improving relationships.

CHAPTER 21

The Capacchione Method

In 1991, I was introduced to a therapeutic process that helped me to understand the workings of my own subpersonalities and bring them into a level of integration and peace. The therapist who was treating me at the time used a form of hypnotherapy to access and work with my subpersonalities, but during this extraordinary period of my own healing I was also introduced to the work of a California-based art therapist named Lucia Capacchione, Ph.D. From her seminal books, The Power of Your Other Hand (1988, 2000), and Recovery of Your Inner Child (1991), I learned a method that allowed me to literally take my healing process into my own two hands. Her method of two-handed writing was to become not only the greatest tool for my own healing process, but also the most valuable tool I have introduced to my clients for their own healing.

Capacchione's method of two-handed writing is deceptively simple and surprisingly effective. There are two reasons that make this method so powerful. The first is that it offers an individual the opportunity to create dialogues with different subpersonalities, providing the relational dynamic that is necessary for creating peace and healing. This is how you can create Socratic dialogues with your subpersonalities. The second reason her method works so well is because two-handed writing requires the activation of both the left and right hemispheres of the brain (see Appendix B for a more detailed explanation of the neurological significance of this process). Using two-handed writing allows you to create new pathways in the forest of your mind, an ability that neurobiologists refer to as neuroplasticity and psychologists refer to as cognitive restructuring. Setting aside the technical jargon, this method can be used to reprogram the mind to think, feel, and behave in new ways. This is a way that you can upgrade the OS of your mind. You are opening up the corpus callosum, a bundle of new fibers, or "phone wires," that connect the hemispheres of the brain and enable them to communicate with each other.

The materials recommended for using the Capacchione method are simply an unlined journal or sketchpad and a set of colored markers or pens. With these materials alone you will be able to practice the dialogue exercises that will be recommended in the following chapters. Even when I explain to my clients how simple and effective this method is, most feel strong apprehensions about trying it. The notions of writing with one's non-dominant hand (the one you don't write with) and having dialogues with oneself are admittedly foreign and odd ones. Gentle encouragement by a therapist is usually enough to get people to try it. When people don't have a therapist to help them get started, they must summon the nerve to try this strange experiment on their own. The upside of doing this on your own is that you needn't worry about anyone else observing or reacting to your effort. If you find yourself curious but reluctant, my recommendation would be to get a copy of one of Capacchione's many fine books to help you break the ice. The hump is a small one to get over, and as soon as most people have their first two-handed dialogue with themselves, awkward discomfort is quickly replaced by something like, "Wow, this is interesting." Consider reading Dr. Capacchione's book, The Creative Journal: The Art of Finding Yourself: 35th Anniversary Edition (2015), to find answers to many questions that may arise.

Another source of apprehension that many people have when getting started with two-handed writing is the fear of what they will discover. The method helps get past psychological defense mechanisms to reach the Heart and subconscious mind, and it can also open the doors to the well-guarded shadow of shame. It's natural to fear the unknown and to hesitate before opening a possible Pandora's Box of distressing thoughts and feelings. This is another reason to consider working with a skilled therapist to ensure that emotional and psychological safety are protected above all else. But this method is actually very well suited for these safeties. To begin with, control lies within your own hands, and thus you are not giving any power or control over to another party. You can stop what you're doing at any point you feel the need to. It's also safe because you will be deciding where and how to direct these conversations with yourself, and you needn't ask any question to which you don't feel prepared to hear the answer. Also contributing to the safety of this method will be the use of the peace skills you've been reading about here. You will not be engaging in arguments with yourself, but instead practicing the skills of respect, understanding, empathy, and nurturance. Think of these dialogues as heart-to-heart talks with a range of characters that are all different parts of yourself. These are the tools for learning how to be loving to yourself, and there is inherent safety in practicing love.

The introductory exercises recommended here are designed to be safe and gentle, and to begin with the safer territories of your psyche. You can wait to address the more complex shadow material of your psyche until you feel safer with the process, or seek professional support when you're ready to venture there. The exercises here are only intended to help readers test the waters rather than begin scuba diving in their minds. You will be the one who decides how far you go, at what pace, and whether to proceed alone or with help.

CHAPTER 22

Peace Talks

Because healing begins with the ability to convert division into wholeness, it's essential to first learn the communication skills for converting conflict into peace. These communication skills can collectively be referred to as *peace talks,* and these will be the subject of this chapter. Peace talks start the process for converting oppositional conflicts into collaborative understandings, and these understandings then become the vehicle that drives the healing and peace process. These dialogue skills are identical to those used by many psychotherapists with their clients, whether they are working with individuals, couples, or families. You will recognize that these dialogues will be free from judgment and will place emphasis on fostering understanding, empathy, and compassion.

These techniques are intended for relationships with those who are not bona fide enemies (though they may sometimes be helpful with enemies under some circumstances), but primarily those with whom you can expect to have personal or civil contacts. They work equally well whether you are dialoguing with others or with your own subpersonalities. For some readers these skills will be familiar and easy to use, especially if they were modeled in their early family life. For others these skills will be less familiar and a greater challenge. This is especially true for those growing up in families where communication and conflict were handled more competitively. Even though practicing this form of communication may cause feelings of awkwardness and vulnerability at first, consider that they are akin to learning how to ride a bike. It may feel unnatural at first, but with a little perseverance and practice it's easily acquired and gets easier with time until it becomes more routine.

The Basics for Peace Talks

Following is a list of the basic ingredients for peace talks, after which they will receive fuller explanation.

1. Make fostering peace in your dialogues with others a priority (intention).
2. Learn to seek, express, and exchange understanding.
3. Learn to suspend judgment.
4. Think win/win instead of win/lose.
5. Adopt a collaborative mindset and language.
6. Make *mutual* understanding your goal.
7. Practice curiosity.
8. Delay solving problems until mutual understandings and empathy are established.
9. Listen and communicate with empathy.
10. Communicate with "I" messages instead of "You" messages.
11. Learn to repeat back the message you hear.
12. Express *concerns* instead of *complaints.*
13. Learn how and when to convey remorse and/or apology.

14. Negotiate new expectations and agreements.
15. Reinforce agreements with recognition and appreciation.

Make fostering peace in your dialogues with others a priority

The natural instinct for dealing with conflict is oppositional (fight or flight). Therefore, it's necessary to recognize and inhibit these tendencies and practice replacing them with a conscious intention to pursue peace. Doing this conveys that you care more about the value of the relationship than your sole interests. This attitude puts others at greater ease and invites them to adopt the same attitude. Learning to guide others into a cooperative mindset that values the relationship will pave the way for all the other ingredients of peace talks to be easier and more effective. A simple question that can foster this alignment is, "Can we find a way to understand each other?" This is not just a question, but an invitation to collaborate.

Learn to seek, express, and exchange understanding

Never underestimate the power of understanding. Many people overlook this in their rush to find solutions to problems and conflicts. But understanding in its own right is immensely helpful. As mentioned in chapter 8, understanding soothes the party being understood, helps the party gaining understanding, and eases the tension between them even before solutions are found. Many problems lack clear solutions but can be made easier to tolerate when there are effective understandings of those problems.

There are three distinct skills to practice in order to gain the full value of understanding. By learning to *seek* understanding from another, you will gain insight that will help you in your relationship with the party you are trying to understand. This is accomplished by activating your curiosity and letting the other party know that you would like his or her help to understand him or her better.

The second skill is to learn how to *express* the understanding that you gain to the party you are coming to understand. Otherwise there is no way for that party to know if you are understanding her or him correctly. Learn how to say, "What I understand you to be saying is…" and then fill in the blank. Be sure to include a description of the emotional element as well as the perception and interpretation of conditions creating that emotion. For example, "I understand that you feel hurt when I don't return your phone calls because it seems to you that I don't care about you."

The third skill is to pursue an exchange of understanding. The most effective way to ask another party to understand you is by offering that party your understanding of them first. People become more understanding once they feel understood themselves. After you seek and express your understanding to another person, ask them if they would be willing to understand your emotions, perception, and interpretation of the circumstance about which you're concerned.

Learn to suspend judgment

Remember that condemning personal judgments are like boomerangs. Because they are weapons that cause harm to others, self, and relationships, they need to be eliminated from peace talks. Practice becoming more mindful of your judgmental reactions and use this awareness to curb their expression. Others can perceive real or imagined judgments in you even when you are careful not to put them into words, as there may be hints of judgment in your tone of voice, body language, or facial expressions. The most effective way to prevent judgments from sabotaging peace talks is by learning how to subdue these reactions internally altogether. This can be accomplished through dialogues with your inner Judge, by practicing mindfulness, and by learning how to empathically discern the motives behind the actions that you are judging.

Think win/win instead of win/lose

True and sustainable peace cannot be won through contest. Ending a battle or a war with a dominating victory may end the contest, but that is not the same as establishing an abiding peace. The Union states defeating the Confederate states ended the US Civil War, but it did not result in true peace between the northern and southern states. True peace can only be accomplished when there can be some form of understanding, negotiation, and new integration between conflicting interests; otherwise resentment and hostility may fester beneath the surface indefinitely.

True peace is won only in partnership and only when the partners show an interest in their relationship, not just their individual interests. This is the difference between zero-sum and non-zero-sum game dynamics. In zero-sum games, a win by one side is matched by a loss on the other side, leaving nothing to be gained for the relationship between the parties. Final score: winner (+1), loser (-1), relationship (either 0 or -1). Non-zero-sum game dynamics occur when the interests of both parties are served simultaneously. Neither side may win all or what it wants, but by making compromises, both sides get part of what they want, plus the benefit of a trustworthy partnership and the peace that comes with that. Final score: party A (+½), party B (+½), relationship (either 0 or +1). The lesson here is that contested outcomes do not serve peace as well as collaborative outcomes.

Adopt a collaborative mindset and language

The easiest and most effective way to get into a collaborative mindset is to adopt the intention to value the peace of the relationship in addition to your individual concerns. This mindset and intention will help guide your language to be less judgmental and competitive. Becoming more mindful of the difference between competitive and collaborative attitudes will also help your communications continue evolving from the former to the latter. The instinct to see yourself as a separate individual who needs to compete or fight for your own interests is extremely powerful, and therefore you'll need patience and persistence before a collaborative mindset and language become second nature to you.

Practice curiosity

When people are on the receiving end of authentic curiosity and a nonjudgmental attitude, you'll find them more willing to open up and share more about what's really going on with them. Even if you think you understand where others are coming from, regardless of whether you're right or wrong, presuming to understand is a mistake. A curious attitude is a caring attitude, and giving others a chance to explain themselves by asking them thoughtful questions is appreciated more than having their minds read. Presuming to understand can reflect a subtle arrogance, while asking for help to understand puts you on a more even footing with others, further reducing tensions.

Delay solving problems until after mutual understanding and empathy are established

There is no doubt that solving problems and resolving conflicts are important for restoring peace. Sometimes a simple fix is all that is needed. But it's important to realize that there is more to managing conflict than finding solutions. There are always two dimensions to consider in a conflict – the *problem* and the *process*. In many conflicts, the problem is not as important as the process is for dealing with it. Whenever a conflict process feels disrespectful, any potential solution for the problem may be unsatisfying unless or until the process becomes more respectful. In other situations there may not be any clear solution to a complicated problem, but when the process for addressing the problem is respectful, the conflict can be greatly eased.

The key to making the conflict process feel respectful is to make understanding and empathy your first priority. These are caring efforts that serve to comfort and gain the trust of others. Doing this first will greatly enhance the prospects for finding potential solutions to the problem at hand.

Imagine that you are in possession of some seeds that you want to plant in your flower garden. You understand that in order for the seeds to germinate, take root, and grow, the soil in your garden must be soft enough to permit these things to happen. Soil that is too densely packed will not allow the seeds to come to fruition. Likewise, if the mind and heart of another are hardened by fear, anger, and distrust, they will not be receptive to the wonderful solutions you may want to introduce. By starting off with understanding and empathy, you prepare their willingness to receive and benefit from solutions. One way to remember this important sequence is to remember the phrase, "Heart-to-heart before head-to-head." Heads will be able to work together best once the hearts are aligned first.

Listen and communicate empathically

Listening and communicating empathically is known as *active listening,* so called because it requires the special effort to understand not just the content of communication, but also the emotional experience that comes with it. If you are preoccupied with your own emotional experience, this will distract you from hearing the complete package of what the other person needs you to understand.

Putting yourself in other people's shoes takes extra time and effort. Empathic listening and communicating requires you to do three things:

1. Pay close *attention* to what the speaker is describing.
2. Imagine being in the speaker's situation in order to feel what she or he is feeling.
3. Explicitly repeat back to the speaker what you understand him or her to be thinking and feeling. It's not enough to simply respond with, "I get it," or, "I hear you." You need to go the distance to fully echo back what the speaker has expressed, and this needs to be done with sincerity.

When you perform active listening effectively, three helpful things occur:

1. The speaker begins to calm down because s/he is feeling listened to and understood.
2. The speaker then becomes better prepared to reciprocate and become an active listener to your point of view.
3. The dynamics of opposition are transformed into the dynamics of collaboration.

Communicate with "I" messages instead of "You" messages

Do not underestimate the different impacts of the words *I* and *You*. The first difference between them is that "I" messages are descriptive, while "You" messages are more likely to be judgmental. *I* messages describe your subjective thoughts, perceptions, emotions, and needs, none of which express the threat of judgment. Therefore, they are safer to listen to and more likely to be respected. *You* messages point a finger toward the listener in ways that are much more likely to trigger defense mechanisms. Regardless of the speaker's intention, using *you* messages in conflict discussions gets perceived as blaming, thereby inviting an oppositional response.

The words that follow *I* messages and *You* messages matter, too. The subjective description of thoughts, perceptions, emotions, and needs are not fighting words. Only when we make declarations or judgments about right and wrong do we set the stage for an argument. For instance, when people hear words like, "you should," or, "you shouldn't," they hear controlling judgments and/or accusations.

The goal of an *I* message is to seek understanding and empathy from the listener, and that means being able to get to the *heart* of your concern. The most effective *I* messages that will connect you and your listener will be those that describe the concerns of your Heart. Voicing your Heart's concern and need is neither judgmental, threatening, nor blaming. Instead of activating the listener's defense mechanisms, messages about the Heart are much more effective at eliciting the empathic understanding of the listener's Nurturer. When both people are able to exchange *I* messages describing their Heart's concerns, and respond with their Nurturer's empathic understandings, conflicts are more than halfway toward being successfully managed.

Learn to repeat back the message that you hear

Once you hear an *I* message from someone, it's important to repeat it back to them in order to demonstrate that you have properly heard and understood the message. Sometimes, we think we've understood the message properly, but upon repeating it back we are informed that we either missed or misunderstood something. To do this effectively, each element of the communication needs to be captured and repeated; the emotion, perception, interpretation, and behavior that triggers each of these elements. The response communication might follow the structure of, "What I hear you saying is that you feel _____ when I do_____ because it seems like _____ and makes you think _____." Therapists refer to this technique as "echoing" or "parroting" a communication back to the speaker, and it's a skill that is fundamental in couples and family therapy. When this is done properly it creates a very comforting experience for the original communicator. The second benefit to repeating these messages back is that it strengthens the understanding in the mind of the person doing the repeating.

Express concerns instead of complaints

The difference between expressing concerns or complaints is just as meaningful as the difference between *I* messages and *You* messages, and for very similar reasons. Complaints are more closely associated with disapproval, criticism, judgment, and blame, thereby activating listeners' defense mechanisms. Concerns are more closely associated with the vulnerability and needs of the Heart, thereby more likely to activate empathic understanding. Just consider the difference between the sound of these two messages;

- *You are* selfish and uncaring because you never bother putting your dishes in the dishwasher.
- *I feel* hurt and worried that you don't care about my feelings when you leave your dishes out.

The *You* message complaint clearly conveys a personal judgment and a presumption of understanding (you don't care). It's the kind of communication most likely to provoke an argument. The *I* message concern describes the subjective experience of the speaker's Heart. While it conveys the worry of not being cared about, the worry is not expressed as an accusation. Imagine how you might react to these messages differently if they were directed toward you.

Know how and when to convey remorse and/or apology

Conflicts create feelings of vulnerability, and it's instinctive to respond to vulnerability by attempting to project strength. On the other hand, expressions of remorse and apology are vulnerable expressions that run counter to one's defensive instincts. When we convey that we feel sorry for how our actions may have caused hurt or harm, we open ourselves up to judgment. If we lack the requisite trust that we can be understood and forgiven, we are less likely to offer these helpful expressions. Only when there is a trust that the relationship matters enough to both partners will it feel safe to do this. Effective apologies help to soften tensions, repair trust, and reinforce caring feelings in both parties.

Negotiating new expectations and agreements

Negotiating new expectations and agreements needs to come near the end-stage of peace talks. Talking about conflicts in a collaborative way that leads to empathic understandings helps till the soil, but the seeds of new agreements must often be planted to finalize conflict management efforts.

Even though humans are innately competitive, we are also wired to relate to one another through fair deals and agreements. We consciously or subconsciously negotiate these deals through tit-for-tat exchanges ("I'll scratch your back if you scratch mine," and, "What goes around, comes around"). The most stable relationships are those in which both parties trust that fair exchanges will be honored. Problems arise when expectations and agreements are not clear enough, because ambiguity allows for different assumptions to be made about what is fair. When this happens, conflicts arise over what adjustments are necessary to restore a sense of fairness and trust. Deciding on what is fair is not always a simple process because fairness can only be determined by weighing a combination of objective and subjective considerations. It may take a lot of negotiating before agreements can be reached that feel fair to both sides, and that is precisely why the process of collaboration and empathic understanding must be created prior to getting to the negotiation of solutions.

In the end, the fairest agreements will be those that both sides regard as combining respect for individual concerns with respect for the relationship itself. It's easier to make individual concessions when they are seen as caring for the other person, serving the relationship, and when similar concessions are being made on the other side.

Reinforce agreements with recognition, appreciation, and praise

New deals and agreements that require changes to behavior can be challenging to keep. New behaviors require time, effort, sacrifice, and perseverance before they become consistent. Therefore they need to be reinforced, and the best forms of reinforcement for new behaviors are the liberal uses of recognition and appreciation. The more often we acknowledge the behaviors we like ("Hey, I noticed that you put the dishes in the dishwasher today"), and the more we express appreciation for new behaviors ("Thank you for doing that for me today"), the more likely that these new behaviors will recur. Don't take agreements for change for granted. It's in the best interests of the relationship for these changes to be encouraged through these simple expressions.

Summary

These fifteen guidelines for peace talks represent skills that are not as natural or instinctive as fight or flight. That means they will be easier to understand than to use on a regular basis. How successful you will be in using them will be greatly influenced by the other party with whom you're using them. Regardless of who that will be, these skills will require practice and plenty of repetition before they will become a well-established upgrade in your mind's operating system, or if you prefer, before these new paths through the forest of your mind become set and automatically travelled.

The good news is that you can practice these peace talk skills within the safety of your own mind by introducing them into the dialogues you'll have with your subpersonalities. Doing so will help you accomplish two goals at the same time. The dialogue exercises in chapter 23 are designed to allow you to begin practicing these new skills while at the same time cultivating more peaceful relationships between your subpersonalities. Using these new skills and new peace accords within your mind will help you create a more peaceful mind for yourself. And, as this new peace is becoming created within your mind, you will begin to notice yourself interacting with other people in increasingly peaceful ways.

CHAPTER 23

Meet and Greet Your Subpersonalities

Until you are able to create peace *within* yourself, your peace with the rest of the world will remain limited. In so many ways, your inner world dictates what your experience with the outer world will be like. That's not to say that the relationship between your inner and outer worlds is a one-way street. The conditions of your outer world have a great impact on your inner world also, especially the lessons imprinted upon you in childhood. Cause and effect travels in both directions. However, you can change *both* your inner and outer world experiences by creating more peaceful conditions in your mind.

The starting point I recommend is to create peace within and between the eight core subpersonalities of your inner family—Judge, Nurturer, Heart, Warrior, Rebel, Ego, Romantic, and Sexual Self. Between these eight parts of your identity, there may be plenty of conflicts and wounds to address. Any conflicts and wounds lying in the shadow territory of your psyche should wait until you take care of your core subpersonalities first. To do this, you will need to begin dialoguing with each of them, then prepare them to dialogue with one another. Although there is no fixed sequence for these dialogues, they will be introduced in a sequence that you may find helpful.

Transforming your core triad

The core triad of your psyche consists of your Heart, Judge, and Nurturer. It's the experience of your Heart that will determine how much happiness and peace you enjoy in your life, and it will be the responsibilities of your Judge and Nurturer (your inner parents) that will have the greatest influence on your Heart's emotional experience. But consider this: *the default dialogue in the subconscious mind of most people involves the Heart hearing the Judge express excessive disapproval, and hearing little to nothing from the Nurturer.* Think about this for a moment. How would you expect a child to feel growing up under those circumstances? This is a formula for emotional misery. Even those who grow up with a strong nurturing influence may lack an internal voice to nurture their Hearts. And, children growing up without harshly critical parents can still end up being more self-critical than self-nurturing. For whatever reason, most people end up with an overabundance of negative self-talk and a deficiency of self-nurturing talk.

The remedy for this imbalance begins with a transformation in the Heart-Judge-Nurturer triad. Specifically, this involves turning down internal judgment, turning up self-nurturing talk, and integrating the functions of control and comfort. This transformation represents a foundational key to inner peace, and therefore should be your highest priority in the exercises that follow.

Once you integrate your Judge and Nurturer, their balanced influence will lead to better care of your Heart and a greater ability to get your other subpersonalities serving your Heart better. In some of the exercises that follow it will be suggested that you use a voice that blends the influences of your Judge and Nurturer together. (If this confuses you, feel free to jump ahead to chapter 24, which further expands on ways to foster the Judge/Nurturer partnership. Then, you can return to the exercises in this chapter with greater clarity.) It's analogous to having two parents form a better partnership to raise a child with the right blend of control and comfort, then managing the other members of the family to contribute to the welfare of the child. This creates a mind in which your Heart, Judge, Nurturer, Warrior, Rebel, Ego, Romantic, and Sexual Self coexist in a more harmonious union.

Preparing to dialogue with your subpersonalities

The dialogue exercises that follow have the potential for opening doors to some powerful emotions, and with this opportunity comes a certain degree of risk. It's recommended that you refer to Appendix A to familiarize yourself with these risks and certain precautions to consider before you proceed.

The exercises are designed for you to have dialogues with your subpersonalities using Capacchione's two-handed writing method. This is not the only method by which cognitive restructuring can be done, but I recommend it because it is by far the easiest and most effective method I've come across in my career. As unusual as it may seem at first, it's actually no more unusual than the notions of riding a bike, or swimming, to the uninitiated. Once you learn these skills they seem perfectly natural.

For each of these dialogue exercises, be guided by the 15 peace talk elements described in chapter 22. Bear in mind, in each of these initial dialogues it will be your conscious/rational mind communicating with your subconscious/*non*-rational mind. What you'll soon discover is that each of your subpersonalities will have their own unique voice for communicating with you. Expect their attitudes, values, beliefs, and language to vary. This is perfectly normal. It will be your conscious/rational mind that will need to take the lead and enlighten them as you proceed. In doing so, your conscious mind will be changing your subconscious mind. This is the process for reprogramming your mind's operating system.

Time to grab your sketch pad and markers. This will work best in a setting that feels safe, relaxed, and as free from distraction as possible.

Greeting your Heart

Remember that your Heart, or Inner Child, represents your emotional sensitivity and emotional needs. Dialoguing with this part of yourself does not mean that you are going back in time to your childhood (although emotional memories from your childhood may emerge when you connect with your Heart). Your Heart is an eternal dimension of your nature, meaning that it's not fixed in time. With this in mind, invite your Heart to select a marker or combination of markers, then draw a picture of herself or himself using your non-dominant hand. Don't worry about the quality of your drawing. This is not an art class where your work is going to be evaluated. Merely try to create a visual representation of your Heart to help your communication experience. It can be a stick figure, a simple face, an elaborate drawing, or anything in between. It doesn't matter. Ask your Judge to take a short nap, then give it a try.

Once you have an image of your Heart to address, let your Heart choose a colored marker to write with using your non-dominant hand. The color doesn't matter or have special meaning other than it's your Heart's preference in the moment. Now, have your Nurturer choose a colored marker with your dominant hand to use in your dialogue with your Heart (unlike the other subpersonalities, dialogues with the Heart work best with the voice of the Nurturer alone, rather than the

Nurture/Judge blend). Begin your dialogue with any of the following questions, or come up with one of your own. Your goal is to invite your Heart into a conversation with you by making him/her feel as safe and cared for as possible.

- Can we talk?
- How are you?
- How are you doing?
- How are you feeling?
- How are you feeling about yourself?

Write your question down at the top of a new page, or on the same page as your drawing if you prefer. Imagine your Heart hearing your question, then take a moment to *listen* for your Heart's reply. Allow your Heart to answer using your non-dominant hand with its chosen marker. Ignore the awkwardness of writing with your non-dominant hand. Expect it to be slower and messier than your dominant hand. Offer the same patience you would to an actual child learning to write you a message for the first time. Value the message more than the form.

However your Heart responds to your question, continue your dialogue with your dominant hand to maintain the connection with your Heart. Be guided by the intention to let your Heart express itself as safely as possible. To do so, you may wish to convey your desire to understand its feelings and needs better. For many people, these initial dialogues with the Heart may feel awkward, especially if there has been a longstanding disconnection or conflict with your emotions. If you sense this awkwardness, proceed as if you have just re-adopted a child whom you had left in an orphanage for a number of years until you were better prepared to care for him/her. Your re-adopted Heart will be experiencing some combination of hunger for loving attention and an anxious guardedness at the same time. The returning parent will need to communicate in ways that convey care and trust. That means learning how to both *lead* and *follow* in these early dialogues. If you encounter silence or excessive guardedness from your Heart at any point, consider asking one of these questions.

- Are you afraid to talk with me?
- Are you uncertain if you can trust me?
- Do you feel worried about talking right now?
- Are you upset with me?

If your Heart begins to open and engage in a dialogue with you, continue for whatever length of time feels comfortable, and be prepared to say goodbye at whatever point you sense your Heart has had enough. Use this opening dialogue to begin establishing trust, conveying care and curiosity to understand your Heart's feelings and needs better. Make establishing trust more important than solving any problem or other goal. You can invite your Heart to ask questions or identify needs that it might have, but you don't need to have answers or solutions at this point. You can still convey to your Heart that you are interested in learning how to protect and care for her or him in new ways.

In the event that your Heart may be reluctant to communicate with you, understand that this is most likely the result of the fear of being judged. If so, consider communicating to your Heart something along these lines:

- I understand that you don't feel comfortable talking with me right now. I'm sorry about that, and I'll try to make things safer so that we can talk more comfortably another time.
- I understand that you may not trust me yet. I'm very sorry about that and I'll work on learning how to earn your trust.

If your Heart still does not feel ready to speak with you, this may indicate that you need to work with your Judge first to create safer conditions for your Heart to open. You can move forward to the exercise for dialoguing with your Judge, then return to your Heart's feelings without judgment.

If your Heart accepts your invitation to dialogue, consider continuing the exchange by asking any of these questions (or others of your own).

- How are you feeling about yourself these days?
- Is there anything making you sad?
- Is there anything making you worried or scared?
- Is there anything you're feeling badly about?
- Is there anything you're needing?
- Is there any way I can help you?
- Are you feeling hurt by any judgments from the inside or outside?

These initial exchanges may reveal things that are disturbing to your Heart's peace. If so, you are learning valuable information that will guide you in the care and healing of your Heart. Solutions will take time to discover and implement. In the meantime, the process of relating to your Heart in a safe, loving way will still be of immeasurable value. Continue having these dialogues with your Heart to practice the skills of non-judgmental curiosity, active listening, and the expression of empathic understanding. Your dominant hand will continue assuming the role of the Nurturer. In the process, your Nurturer will be practicing and honing his or her new skills.

When you finish a dialogue with your Heart, find a way of saying goodbye with words of affection, appreciation, reassurance, and your intention to return. Here are some examples that will convey to your Heart how much you value it.

- Thank you for talking with me.
- I look forward to us talking again.
- I'm glad that I can understand your feelings better now.
- I want to learn how to take better care of you.
- I'm sorry that I don't have a solution yet, but I will seek help to figure this out, and will stay with you in the meantime.
- I'll be back soon to talk with you more.
- I love you!

If you find yourself feeling anxious about your ability to help your Heart with its significant sufferings and needs, this is normal. Your loving intentions and efforts will still be enormously comforting to your Heart. You don't need to have all the answers or abilities to meet your Heart's needs, just as no parent can meet all the needs of their child(ren) alone. All good parents have limitations and are willing to seek help from others when necessary. Whatever needs your Heart reveals that you don't know how to meet, you can pursue help for from someone who does have the skills to help.

Addressing your Judge

In many ways your Judge is the captain of your destiny. For most people, the Judge determines the structure of your value system and exerts a controlling influence over your personal and interpersonal behavior. *Your life cannot be transformed in any way unless your Judge condones the changes you wish to make.* The exercises here will help you get started with your Judge, laying the groundwork for further upgrades to its control program.

Many people experience great discomfort anticipating communication with their Judge. This apprehension may involve fear, guilt, anger, or even hatred. That's because the Judge represents the ultimate authority in the mind, and this authority is vested with dominant power, too often used in hurtful ways.

Take a moment to consider what it is that your Judge is expected to accomplish in your life. It must control all of your primitive impulses, urges, and desires. It has pushed you to finish your homework, meet the boss' expectations, pay the bills, get the chores done, and parent the child(ren). The Judge is responsible for meeting social standards, keeping you out of trouble with the authorities, keeping you healthy, and enforcing all manner of rules, demands, and duties. Also consider who taught your Judge to perform these tasks: parents, teachers, clergy, coaches, bosses, and other authorities in your life. Has it always been loving? Probably not. These are thankless and difficult responsibilities. Some of your subpersonalities have made these responsibilities hard for your caretakers in the past, and now they are hard for your Judge. The Judge has to manage the defiant Rebel, the aggressive Warrior, the oversensitive Heart, the blind Romantic, the competitive Ego, and the lustful Sexual Self. Is it any wonder that your Judge may have become a loud, angry, critical, demanding, shaming tyrant inside your head? That's who you're preparing to dialogue with, so you are entitled to be more than a little uneasy about it.

Keep this in mind as you approach your Judge — **even though your Judge is the ruling authority in your life, s/he is also your most important servant.** Just as a captain is the commander of all those aboard the ship, the captain and crew are all intended to serve the welfare of the most important passenger aboard — your Heart. Collectively, the Judge's services require a great deal of controlling authority to be successful. Therefore, it's important to recognize the difference between your Judge's harsh *methods* and its loving *purpose*. If your Judge's methods are hurtful, that is simply due to poor training or the absence of good training. Whatever the reason, Judges that are most anxious tend to become the most harsh in their methods.

Still, such Judges can be re-trained to serve their functions in more benevolent ways, provided they are approached with the respect they deserve in their role.

Your primary goal in your initial dialogues with your Judge is to earn its trust so that you can build a collaborative relationship with this important captain. *Your key to greater peace relies on being able to establish a collaborative relationship with your Judge for the sake of changing your mind.* Once you do so, your ship's captain can chart a new course toward a more peaceful life.

When you're ready, have your Judge pick a marker with your non-dominant hand, then you pick another with your dominant hand to use in the dialogue. Next, choose one of the following questions to write down to address your Judge with your dominant hand.

- Can we talk?
- How do you feel about how our life is going?
- Do you have concerns about me?
- What do you think about our Heart?
- Are you trying to hurt me or trying to help me?
- Do you recognize some of the ways you can be hurtful to me?
- Are there parts of me that you have concerns about?
- Are you willing to consider new ways of helping me that might be less hurtful?

As with your Heart, make your initial goal to have a safe and respectful dialogue with your Judge. Don't be concerned with solving problems or convincing your Judge to change its ways right off the bat. Instead, focus on the goal of developing mutual respect, trust, and empathic understandings. Your Judge will only consider what you have to say if you demonstrate respect for its authority. If you want to ask your Judge to understand your concerns, you must first demonstrate your willingness to understand your Judge's concerns first.

After breaking the ice with your Judge, consider asking what concerns s/he has about your other seven subpersonalities. This interview with your Judge might be quite revealing. Wherever your Judge has concerns will point the way toward where more peace is needed. These will be the areas where your Judge is working hardest to exert control, resulting in conflicts between your Judge and any subpersonalities with whom it's concerned. Like your opening dialogues with your Heart, this is in some ways a fact finding mission to uncover where peace and healing are needed.

In every dialogue with your Judge, remain clear that you want to support the Judge's job rather than undermine it. But you are also there to consult with your Judge about ways it can do its job peacefully for your Heart and the rest of your inner family. Your role is to support and collaborate. Whenever you finish a dialogue with your Judge, express your gratitude to her/him for listening to you, responding to you, and collaborating with you. If, for any reason, you find yourself at an impasse with your Judge, consider seeking support from a therapist to help you work through the block.

Engaging the Nurturer

Now it's time to get better acquainted with the second parent in your psyche, your inner Nurturer. Your Nurturer's role is to bring emotional comfort to your Heart and any other subpersonality of your inner family that is distressed. The Nurturer can also be quite helpful for soothing conflicts between different subpersonalities. If your Nurturer hasn't been performing these tasks adequately for you, there are two likely reasons for this. Either you have not acquired effective skills for nurturing, or you have these skills but only use them to serve the needs of others. At the risk of reinforcing a stereotype, men usually suffer from the former, and women from the latter. Frequently, males are taught to believe that nurturing is feminine by nature, while females are often taught to be self-sacrificing nurturers. Both of these imbalances need to be corrected.

Too often the role of the Nurturer is devalued, if not completely denigrated. Those who are in need of nurturance may also be ridiculed. These attitudes interfere with the adequate development and use of nurturing skills. Sometimes, parents may offer nurturance while their children are young, then begin withholding it as they become adolescents or young adults, conveying the message that it should no longer be necessary. Whatever the case, consider the possibility that your Nurturer has not received the respect or appreciation that it deserves. Keep these observations in mind as you prepare to engage with your Nurturer and empower it to serve your needs more effectively.

Have your Nurturer choose a colored marker with your non-dominant hand, then you choose another with your dominant hand. Consider starting with one of the following questions:

- How are you holding up?
- Are you feeling valued?
- Are you feeling burdened? By what or whom?
- Do you feel as though you know how to nurture effectively?
- How do you feel about caring for our Heart's needs?
- Is there anything you're needing?
- Is there anything you're concerned about?
- How do you think others will react to you if you need to set limits and say "no" more often?
- How do you think others will respond if you start taking better care of our Heart's feelings and needs?
- How do you think others will respond if you expect them to take care of their own feelings and needs more?
- How do you feel about talking directly with our Heart?
- How do you feel about our Judge?

- How do you feel about communicating with our Judge to develop a better partnership with him/her for the sake of managing our inner family more effectively?
- Are there other subpersonalities causing concern for you?

It may take repeated dialogues with your Nurturer before you can empower her/him to have a stronger partnership with your Judge and a greater influence on the peace of your inner family. Again, make the building of a collaborative relationship with your Nurturer the first priority of your dialogues. The specifics of how it will learn to better serve you will evolve over time.

One critical issue that many people need to work out with their Nurturers is the question of selfishness. Many people are taught to love (and nurture) others *instead* of loving (and nurturing) themselves because they believe the latter is selfish. This is completely untrue. This misconception arises from the confusion between selfishness and *self-care*, egotism and *self-esteem*, self-centeredness and *self-preservation*. In order for Nurturers to best give to others, the needs of one's own Heart must first be satisfied. Caring for oneself in no way conflicts with caring for others, but is instead a prerequisite for it. Keep this in mind as you seek to encourage your Nurturer to improve the balance and peace in your life.

Consulting with your Warrior

All that is required for getting in touch with your inner Warrior is to follow your anger. Anger is the emotional energy that your Warrior uses to protect you from anything perceived as a threat. It mobilizes your aggressive instincts to oppose or conquer threats. That makes your Warrior a valuable ally for self-preservation. Problems can arise whenever a Warrior's reactions are out of balance or control. This could mean there is either too much protective anger, not enough protective anger, or protective anger expressed in ways that backfire and make things worse (winning a battle but losing the war).

Most of us don't receive enlightened training for how to use our Warrior's anger safely and effectively. That leaves us at the mercy of our instincts and what we observe from our parents and other formative influences. Males and females are taught different lessons about what to do with anger. For girls and women, anger is frequently denigrated by referring to it as "bitchiness." For boys and men, anger is too often glorified as a sign of power, courage, and dominance. Both sets of cultural distortions about anger serve to make conflict management worse rather than better.

The secret to optimal peace and safety lies in the *judicious* use of anger. For your Warrior to protect you best, you'll want it to be able to set limits with resolve and convey properly measured warnings of consequence without going too far in provoking escalations of hostility. This advice is unavoidably vague, because all conflict dynamics are different depending on who is involved and what is at stake. Therefore, your dialogues with your Warrior are best guided by the recognition that self-defense needs to be guided more by reflective thinking than reactive impulses.

As you begin your dialogue with your Warrior, bear in mind that you are communicating with an honorable ally. Even if you are extremely displeased with how your Warrior goes overboard, or not far enough to protect you, understand this is only a consequence of inadequate training. You can retrain your Warrior to serve and protect you better, however, to do so you'll need to engage it respectfully. This can be accomplished by accessing the right voice (part Judge, part Nurturer), when you interact with your Warrior. Chapter 24 will further expand on how to blend the voices of your Judge and Nurturer.

With your sketchpad and markers, have your Warrior choose a marker with your non-dominant hand, and have your Judge/Nurturer voice choose another with your dominant hand. Consider one of the following questions for connecting with your Warrior.

- How's it going?
- Is there anyone or anything you're mad at these days?
- How's the fight?
- Are you mad about anything in particular?
- Are there any situations disturbing your sleep these days?
- How do you feel about the job you're doing these days?
- Is there anything you're regretting?
- Are there other subpersonalities that you're unhappy with?
- Do you understand why I have some concerns about the ways you protect me?
- Would you be open to exploring new ways you can protect me that might have fewer negative consequences?

Another option for supporting your Warrior is to invite her or him to do an "anger dump." This simply means asking your Warrior to write a list of *everything* s/he is mad about that comes to mind. The list might be extensive and overwhelming. That's okay, because this exercise is only for the purpose of venting, not fixing. If you try this exercise, simply respond to your Warrior's list with sincere empathy. You might say something like, "Wow, that's intense, and I can understand all these reasons for being so mad. I'll do whatever I can to support you." Even without any solution or action taken, this dialogue can release a lot of pent-up tension and make you feel better.

Whichever exercise you choose for connecting with your Warrior, focus the process on respect, understanding, trust, empathy, and collaboration rather than on problem solving. Making changes to fix problematic patterns can be complicated, slow, and sometimes require help from others. Finding solutions and learning to implement them will depend heavily upon your ability to change the nature of your relationship with your Warrior first. That means that instead of your Warrior operating independently on instinct and autopilot, you are now partnering with your Warrior as a guiding consultant. This brings the benefits of your rational mind to the subconscious program that directs your Warrior's actions. By doing so, you can teach your Warrior the difference between anger and hostility, assertiveness and aggression. No matter what defense mechanisms you learn to employ going forward, they will benefit from this reflective collaboration between your conscious and subconscious minds. A Warrior that benefits from reflective thinking will be more effective than one that is merely reactive.

See how far you can go by having supportive dialogues with your Warrior on your own. As long as you see things evolving, continue with what you're doing. If you find yourself getting stuck over how to improve the effectiveness of your defense mechanisms, consider seeking the help of a good therapist who is familiar with anger management and assertiveness training.

Ego

People have very different feelings about their Egos, either loving them, hating them, or having conflicted feelings about them. Many religious and spiritual disciplines identify the Ego of selfish pride and attachment as the root of suffering and other evils. There is some truth to this. But as mentioned in chapter 11, the Ego has both a virtue and a curse side to it, just like every other subpersonality. In the competitive realms of society where we strive for recognition, respect, rank, and access to resources, we need the Ego to serve us in these contests. But, as with all other subpersonalities, the Ego must play its part in a balanced, well-regulated way in order to not make life harder than it needs to be. Some Egos need to be reined in, and others may need more praise. Either way, to regulate your Ego means developing the same collaborative alliance with it that you build with all your other subpersonalities.

With your sketchpad and markers, have your Ego choose a color with your non-dominant hand, and your Judge/Nurturer voice choose a color with your dominant hand. Select one of the following questions to get your dialogue with your Ego under way.

- How are you feeling about yourself these days?
- Tell me some things that you feel proud of.
- Is there anyone you're feeling threatened by lately?
- Are there parts of us that make you feel inferior or inadequate?
- Are you aware of some of the ways you make other people feel uncomfortable?
- How do you feel about other people who act superior?
- Can we discuss ways that you can feel proud without making others feel threatened?
- Are there other subpersonalities threatening your sense of pride?
- How do you feel about our sensitive Heart?

In your dialogues with your Ego, your goal is to moderate its patterns rather than attempting to eliminate them, because as long as you are a part of a competitive society, you will need the Ego's service. One of the principle goals of regulating your Ego is to help it understand the importance of protecting your Heart-centered relationships. Over-inflated Egos frequently trample on the feelings of others and interfere with one's own emotional needs being met. Therefore it's often important for the Ego to learn to honor the priority of the Heart's needs for self and others. The Ego must play a supportive role in your life, not a dominant one.

Another matter that many people may need to address with their Egos is a difference between being *proud* and being *arrogant*. Pride is an experience that can be shared with the Heart in order to develop a healthy self-esteem. Arrogance, on the other hand, conveys a sense of superiority that may offend, hurt, and/or provoke anger in others. Arrogance is a type of disrespect that conveys the message, "I am superior; you are inferior." One of the most important antidotes for arrogance is a well-maintained sense of humility. Over-identifying with your Ego diminishes the extent to which you can stay in touch with your emotional and/or spiritual needs. This balance influences how you relate to others. People respond to competitive, egotistical and arrogant personalities much differently than they do to Heart-centered personalities or those emanating the humility of a spiritual nature. This is not an A or B choice, because it's entirely possible to have a blend of Ego pride and personal humility that allows us to regard others as our equals on a human level.

The Rebel

The Rebel can be responsible for disturbing a lot of peace for self and others. When poorly regulated, Rebels often provoke fear, anger, and punishments from others. It's always unfortunate when a Rebel undermines its own cause as a result of its misguided efforts. Like the Ego, the Rebel is a valuable subpersonality to preserve and guide, rather than to extinguish. It will require respect, understanding, and collaborative guidance before it will consider modifying its ways, because Rebels absolutely *hate* to feel controlled. Rebels favor freedom and independence above all else. These are great virtues for your Rebel to bring into your life. But it must also be understood that freedom and independence need to be balanced with getting along with others, and this requires learning to live with rules, compromises and other forms of agreement.

Communicating with your Rebel will be an enormous test of the partnership between your Judge and Nurturer, just as there is a natural antagonism between rebellious teenagers and their parents. Your Nurturer may need to help your Judge refrain from scolding, lecturing, or offending the Rebel with disapproval. The collaboration between your team of inner parents and your Rebel is an important and delicate process that may require time to modify (especially if your Rebel has lost control with alcohol and/or drugs that further destabilize the chances for a sustained balance). For some people, the Rebel will need to be reined in for a healthier balance between freedom and control. For others, the Rebel may need to be empowered to exercise more freedom and independence if there is an imbalance in the opposite direction (if living under excessive control from self or others). The relationship between control and freedom in your life can result from either a *competition* or a *collaboration* between these values. Healthier and more peaceful balances are always best served by the collaborative process, so let this understanding guide you in your dialogues with your Rebel.

Rebels like the freedom to choose as well as the freedom to swear. Let your Rebel choose whatever damn color it prefers with whichever damn hand it wants for dialoguing with you. Let your Judge/Nurturer pick a color to use with your other hand. Then, choose whichever questions feel right from the following list to start dialoguing with your Rebel:

- Are you getting the respect you deserve?
- How are you feeling treated these days?
- What do you think of our Judge?
- Are there other parts of our inner family that are bothering you?
- Who is there in our life these days that bothers you the most?
- Are there circumstances in our life that you would like to see change?

- Are you needing more independence or freedom in any way?
- How do you feel about the needs and vulnerabilities of our Heart?
- Are you willing to take our Heart's needs into consideration as we look for the right balance between freedom and control in our life?

Use your dialogues with your Rebel to build mutual understanding, respect, empathy, trust, and a growing partnership to best suit the welfare of your inner family as a whole.

The Romantic

Your Romantic is moved by ideals, not just in love, but in anything it may feel passionate about. Passions can be marvelous and rewarding to pursue. They can just as easily land us in trouble and result in heartbreak. This is because the passions of the Romantic are often intoxicating in their extremes. When your Romantic gets swept away by a passion, it may lose the perspective necessary to recognize and avoid danger. Sadly, when there are heartbreaking consequences from these blinding passions, the Romantic may end up getting shut down altogether by the Judge because it will come to be regarded as untrustworthy. In order for the Romantic to be a valuable member of your inner family, you'll need to help it find the right balance between idealism and realism, what is possible and what is probable, and to discern the benefits and risks of going out on various limbs in life.

With your sketchpad and markers, have your Romantic choose a color with your non-dominant hand, and allow your Judge/Nurturer to choose one with your dominant hand. Consider which of the following questions might be useful for starting your dialogues with your Romantic:

- Tell me about your dreams.
- How do you feel about our pursuit of your dreams at this point in our life?
- Are there any mistakes that you're regretting?
- How confident do you feel about your dreams?
- How hopeful are you feeling about love (or some other passion)?
- Can you recognize some of the ways we have been too careful or too careless?
- How do you feel about working together to find the right balance between our ideals and the realities of life?
- Do you have concerns that you'd like me to understand?
- Are there other subpersonalities that are interfering with fulfilling your desires?

Use your dialogues with your Romantic to examine the balance between its needs and the needs of the rest of your inner family. Let your Romantic know that you want to support its needs and desires, while also asking it to understand your other concerns for emotional safety. Working together collaboratively will help you find the balance that is best for you.

Sexual Self

Your Sexual Self will be the least rational subpersonality to partner with and regulate. Depending on your life experience, age, gender, and sexual orientation, your Sexual Self may be out of balance in either direction – overcontrolled or undercontrolled. Because shame is the most common force used to regulate sexuality, your Sexual Self may need help being freed from shame if it's overcontrolled. If your Sexual Self is undercontrolled, you'll need to rein it in without resorting to the use of shame. Either way, regulating your Sexual Self will once again call on the best teamwork your Judge/Nurturer hybrid can muster. You'll want your sexuality to be adequately controlled while also remaining comfortable with itself. Use your dialogues with your Sexual Self to develop mutual understanding about its needs and those of the rest of your inner family.

With sketchpad and pens, use your dominant hand to invite your Sexual Self into a dialogue, beginning with any question(s) that might help you best address your concerns. Here are some options that might help you get started:

- Are you feeling satisfied these days?
- Do you feel frustrated or disappointed sexually?
- How are you feeling about your sexuality?
- Do you feel hurt by shame?
- How well do you feel I'm meeting your needs and desires?
- How do you feel our partner is meeting your needs and desires?
- Do you feel comfortable talking about sex with me?
- Do you feel comfortable talking about sex with our partner?
- Do you understand the need for certain limits to be imposed upon your desires?

Regulating sexuality can be complicated and delicate, whether that involves reining it in, liberating it, or some of each. Your chances of doing this successfully will depend upon establishing a reasonable collaboration with this very *non*-reasonable part of your nature. If you find yourself getting stuck in this effort, look for counsel from a trustworthy and wise source. If you take good care of your Sexual Self, it will add immeasurable benefits to your life.

Summary

Remember that these are introductory dialogues with your eight core subpersonalities, and as such are only meant to help you get acquainted with them, get acquainted with the two-handed writing method, and discover sources of distress and conflict in your mind. In addition, you are focusing on building foundations of trust and collaboration with each of your subpersonalities. You can return to having more dialogues with your subpersonalities after learning more about how to care for them from the lessons that will be described in chapter 25. Allow yourself to be patient with the process. Changing your mind on the subconscious level is an important undertaking that deserves great care and persistence.

CHAPTER 24

New Leadership

If you have tried the exercises in chapter 23, you may now have greater insight about the contours and contents of your subconscious mind. The more you dialogue with your subpersonalities, the more you will learn about the sources of pain, imbalance, and conflict existing among them. These discoveries will shed light on why you are lacking the peace and wholeness of mind you desire, and they will guide you toward where peace needs to be made. The process is similar to a family therapist interviewing all the members of a family to discover where the sources of suffering are, and then using this information to guide your interventions. For you, the family is the collection of your subpersonalities and you are their therapist.

Perhaps you're wondering, "How can I be a therapist to my family of subpersonalities?" This chapter is going to help you develop the skills for doing just that. This may not eliminate your need to find a professional therapist, but it will teach you how to do much of the work for yourself. And to do so, *you will need to create a new form of leadership in your mind*.

The problems of imbalanced control

Why do you need new leadership for your mind? Because, if you're like the majority of people, the default leadership in your subconscious is out of balance. With the Judge and Nurturer representing the two parent roles in the psyche, too often the Judge's influence dominates over that of the Nurturer. Most people's internal control relies on the use of criticism, judgment, guilt, and shame, and it lacks the tempering influences of understanding, empathy, compassion, forgiveness, and affirmation. It's analogous to a family dominated by an authoritarian parent and lacking a comforting parent.

There are several problems with having such an imbalanced inner control system. First, even though a domineering Judge can be effective for controlling behavior, it often causes great misery in the process. This might take the form of anxiety, depression, anger, or stress-induced health problems. In other words, your well-being can be sacrificed when the mechanisms of control are excessively harsh.

Another problem resulting from overly authoritarian control is that it often contributes to various forms of instability. Obedience in response to excessive fear, guilt, or shame often generates rebellious impulses. Any circumstance that is grossly out of balance becomes vulnerable to pendulum swings, both small and large. Consider an individual who is tightly controlled by the demands of daily life and turns to alcohol or drugs to unwind after a grueling day or week. With excessively rigid control, it becomes more likely that alcohol and drugs will be misused and trigger a backlash. Mood and behavioral swings may become reckless and destructive. Another example of the instability resulting from imbalanced control is the proverbial mid-life crisis. When an individual spends the first half of his or her life rigidly governed by imbalanced programs, this can lead to a breaking point in which that person feels an overwhelming need to break free and start life over on new terms. Marriages, families, and careers are sometimes sacrificed in the throes of a such crisis. These are examples of how imbalanced forms of control contribute to instabilities in life.

A third problem with an over reliance on the authoritarian use of fear, guilt, and shame is that it inhibits the processes of growth, transformation, and healing. These are processes that rely on the exercise of free will, and free will is a frequent casualty of authoritarian rule. Thinking and deciding for oneself become a danger when control is autocratic. In order to create meaningful change in your life, there needs to be adequate permission and safety to take risks, make mistakes, and discover new possibilities for change. Imbalanced control stifles transformational experiences.

If you are one of the millions of individuals who are too hard on yourself, or if you tend to be your own worst enemy, then you may need a new internal control experience that is more balanced. Your mind may need new leadership.

The reasons for imbalances between control and comfort

The historic conflict between the values of control and comfort literally has biblical proportions. The Old Testament of the Bible largely embodies the elements of God's laws. This collection of writings includes the Ten Commandments and detailed stories about the fate of those who abide by or violate those Commandments. The Old Testament represents the Judge side of God's nature, responsible for teaching us all how to behave in accordance with God's will. The New Testament, by contrast, reflects the Nurturer side of God's nature through His gifts of compassion, mercy and forgiveness. These two presentations of God's nature have caused a great deal of confusion and conflict among the faithful. Some Christian denominations place greater emphasis on adhering to God's laws, while others emphasize God's compassionate nature more. Many make efforts to balance the two. Efforts to reconcile the two sides of God's word have been the subject of great theological debate for centuries. The words of Jesus provided an enigmatic hint about the relationship between the two sides of God's nature when he said, "I have not come to abolish the law, but to fulfill it" (Matthew 5:17 KJV). This is no more a Christian confusion than it is for all other religious, atheist, and secular thinkers. In order for any mind to find greater peace, the relationship between control and comfort needs to be better understood, integrated and balanced.

In the modern era, confusion about the relationship between control and comfort is recognized in the controversy over the difference between *conditional love* and *unconditional love*. Conditional love is understood as an approval that is earned by meeting the various expectations held by those from whom you seek love. Earning this form of love requires you to conform to specific values held by others who are important to you. In contrast, unconditional love is not something that is earned. When a newborn comes into the world, the love that s/he is showered with has nothing to do with looks, talent, intelligence, or behavior. This is a love that is given entirely for free. It's free from any conditional terms. Should there be a time when unconditional love comes to an end and then be replaced by conditional love? If so, when? Or, can it be possible to sustain unconditional love toward our children and others, even while we express more conditional approval and disapproval at the same time? The answer to this question will ultimately determine how your Judge and Nurturer work together, and how they will then relate to others (within and without).

How is a Judge expected to exert control when love is granted freely? One can hear this question being asked by many authoritative parents to their spouses who emphasize nurturance ahead of discipline. "You'll spoil the children if you love them unconditionally!" A nurturing spouse might reply by saying, "We can't love our children only according to how well they obey us!" This debate captures the essential divide between control and comfort, a divide that can be so great as to destroy some marriages and undermine the goal of raising well-adjusted children.

In order for you to have a peaceful, well-regulated mind, your own Judge and Nurturer must find ways to heal their divide and forge a marriage between the values of control and comfort. For this to happen, the misconceptions about the nature of unconditional love need to be cleared up.

Conditional love and unconditional love are neither contradictory nor mutually exclusive. They can, and must, coexist in your own mind and in your relationships with others. It cannot be one or the other, or one against the other. It needs to be one *with* the other. To understand how this is possible, recognize that they have entirely different targets and purposes. The target for conditional love is *behavior*, and its purpose is to regulate behavior. The target for unconditional love is the Heart, and its purpose is to maintain peace and comfort in the Heart. ***It is entirely possible, and necessary, to love the Heart of a person freely, while at the same time letting that person know that their behavior must be controlled in order to be acceptable.*** There should be no confusion in the message, "I love you no matter what, but your behavior must be acceptable to receive my approval." Or, "Just because I need to discipline your behavior doesn't mean that I don't love you."

Everyone needs to be the recipient of both conditional and unconditional love. All children need to be controlled while simultaneously being assured that they will always be loved. Unconditional love in the absence of control will spoil a child. Conversely, command over a child's behavior in the absence of compassion will damage a child's spirit. This is the essential understanding that your own Judge and Nurturer must agree to for them to heal their divide. This is the understanding they will need in order for them to form a marriage of values between control and comfort.

Enter a new "Conductor"

Imagine being hired to conduct an orchestra of teenage musicians from around the world. Each possesses enough skill to qualify for your orchestra, but much more than skill will be required for them to make harmonious music as a group. Being teenagers with contrasting backgrounds and values, their behavior will need to be controlled and their relationships with one another will need to be supported. Orchestras don't have two conductors – one for control and the other for comfort. A single conductor must combine those skills to accomplish both goals. As their conductor, you must teach them to comply with your direction, at the same time helping them forge a unified identity and purpose. This is the only way they will be able to perform harmoniously.

Managing your subconscious mind is very similar to conducting an orchestra. The different subpersonalities all need to follow the lead of a conductor that embodies the skills of control and comfort.

In chapter 10, different controllers of the subconscious were associated with different theoretical models. In Freudian psychoanalysis, it was called the Ego. In Berne's Transactional Analysis, it was called the Adult. And, in Schwartz's Internal Family Systems model, it was called the Self. The term that I use for this role is Conductor, for the reasons mentioned above. Most of your self-control requires a blend of control and comfort, and one blended voice can do this more effectively than two independent voices.

Introducing the Conductor as a subpersonality does not mean that your Judge and Nurturer cease to exist as independent subpersonalities.

Some circumstances may require control without special need for comfort, and others may call for comfort without need for control. For managing the imbalances and conflicts of your subpersonalities, the best results come from a unified voice that incorporates both. That unified voice will henceforth be referred to as your Conductor.

Create your Conductor by marrying your Judge and Nurturer

If you understand these explanations, that's an important start. However, understanding alone will not be enough to heal the divide and forge the marriage between your Judge and Nurturer. Remember, healing is a *relational* process, not something that comes from rational comprehension alone. For this to occur, your Judge and Nurturer must actually dialogue with one another until they can merge their value systems. If two divided parents both read the same book that explains the importance of conditional and unconditional love, they will not automatically become better partners in parenting. To do so, they would need to talk about the subject and agree to work together to blend these two forms of love. The same is true for your Judge and Nurturer.

Reaching the goal of bringing healing and peace to your mind hinges upon your ability to merge your Judge and Nurturer. Whatever imbalances or wounds exist in any of your subpersonalities, they cannot be effectively addressed until your Judge and Nurturer can address them as a team. The same is true for addressing conflicts between subpersonalities. The healing of individual subpersonalities, and their relationships with each other, must be addressed through the partnership of your Judge and Nurturer.

In order to develop an effective Conductor, your Judge and Nurturer need to dialogue to create a cohesive partnership. Think of it like a perfect marriage between the providers of control and comfort (gender being irrelevant). The word *gestalt* is defined as an organized whole that is perceived as greater than the sum of its parts. The unified Conductor is greater than the Judge and Nurturer when they are functioning independently. Children raised by conflicted parents providing control and comfort do not benefit as much as children raised by parents united in these roles. When they are whole, they are greater than when they are independent.

Another important reason for the partnership between the Judge and the Nurturer is that the Nurturer possesses skills for enlightening the Judge and motivating it to change. The Nurturer's empathy is necessary for understanding the feelings and needs of every sub-personality in the psyche. The Nurturer's considerate and respectful use of language makes it easier for the Judge to understand and be receptive to new perspectives.

The secret to forming an effective partnership between your Judge and Nurturer will be for them to use their dialogues to develop mutual understanding and respect for their roles. To get this process underway, grab your sketch pad and markers. For these dialogues, it's not important which hands you use for which role. Follow your intuition or let them decide. It doesn't matter who starts the dialogue, though a rule of thumb is to start your dialogues with your dominant hand. Consider one of the following questions to get them started, or let them choose their own way to start:

- How do you feel about the idea of working together as partners?
- How do you feel about the way I'm doing my job?
- Are there changes you'd like me to consider for me to do my job better?
- Do you understand my role?
- Do you respect the importance of my role?
- Do you have any concerns about how we can work together?
- How can I earn your trust?

As you allow the dialogues between your Judge and Nurturer to unfold, notice the tone and tenor of their communications. Does it sound respectful, understanding, and cooperative? Do you hear or sense tension between them? If necessary, refer back to the elements of peace talks in chapter 22 to see if there's anything that might help them improve their alliance. Encourage them to express understanding and appreciation for one another. Help them become partners in a unified voice of new leadership. Together, let them become your new Conductor.

CHAPTER 25

How to Heal and Create Peace Within

You have met and become acquainted with your core family of sub-personalities. You have begun creating a new Conductor to lead your inner family using an integrated blend of control and comfort. Now, it's finally time to heal and create peace within your mind.

In this chapter, six elements of healing and peacemaking are described for you to use in your future dialogues. Each element can be used with any and every subpersonality in need. You can also use your skills to heal and create peace between different subpersonalities that may be in conflict with one another. The six elements that will be described for healing and creating peace are:

1. Expressing
2. Understanding
3. Comforting

4. Balancing
5. Managing conflicts
6. Healing

If the prospect of using these six elements with and between all your subpersonalities sounds a bit ambitious, that's because it is. This chapter is not going to walk you through the whole range of potential wounds, imbalances, and conflicts within your psyche, as that would be another book unto itself. Instead, the basic process for using these elements will be described along with some sample dialogue exercises that will help you get your healing and peace-making journey under way. For the most part, the dialogues recommended in this chapter will be guided by your Conductor using your dominant hand. However, there may be comfort dialogues that call for the voice of your Nurturer alone. Then, there will be dialogues taking place between subpersonalities in conflict that won't necessarily include the voice of your Conductor.

Expressing

Whenever someone is experiencing emotional distress of any form, it's a loving gift to invite them to simply express their feelings to you freely. Your subpersonalities will appreciate this also. The first lesson about this gift is that the expression of emotion can be very relieving in itself. Sometimes we just need to vent. Receiving understanding in response to venting is even better. Once again, practice separating the impulse to fix problems from this opportunity to express. *Even if you recognize distortions in perception, reasoning, or logic, don't let that interfere with the need to let emotions be expressed without interference.*

Let one of your subpersonalities that might be in distress take a colored marker with your non-dominant hand, and have your

Conductor choose one with your other hand. Your Conductor can begin this dialogue by simply asking, "Is there anything you'd like to get off your chest?" Whatever it might be, just let that subpersonality let it rip in whatever language feels natural. Don't interrupt unless you are inviting the subpersonality to elaborate or express more. When you notice distortions in perception, interpretation, or logic, or when you see a contrasting point of view, file it away for a later dialogue. This current dialogue is only intended to help a subpersonality gain comfort by letting go of tension. Opportunities for engaging the mind to solve problems can wait.

After your subpersonality finishes its expression, have your Conductor respond with a statement of understanding and empathy. Pay attention to how that changes the way you feel, both emotionally and physically. Have your Conductor thank the subpersonality for sharing important emotion and thought. Perhaps the subpersonality may express gratitude for the gift, which is good for the relationship between the subpersonality and the Conductor. If you feel the need, your Conductor might end with, "I recognize this is a concern that you may need some help with, and I'm willing to talk with you another time to see if we can figure something out." Practice this exercise with any subpersonality you sense might benefit from it, letting the voices of worry, fear, sadness, frustration, anger, fury, despair, guilt, or shame have a chance to unload.

Understanding

Dialogues of understanding with your subpersonalities will serve three purposes for you. The first is that they will help you understand your subpersonalities better. The second is that the understanding you respond with will provide them with greater comfort. And the third is that understanding will improve the relationships between your subpersonalities and your Conductor.

To get the hang of this type of dialogue, pick a subpersonality that you might like to understand better (Heart, Warrior, Rebel, Ego, Sexual Self, Romantic). Let that subpersonality choose a colored marker with your non-dominant hand, then have your Conductor choose one with your dominant hand. Imagine sitting down with that subpersonality for a heart-to-heart chat and have your Conductor find a way to initiate the dialogue. Simple lines to get started with are: "Can we talk?", "How're you doing?" or, "I'd like to understand you better, can you help me with that?" Feel free to use your own style of communicating, and tailor it to the nature of the subpersonality you're dialoguing with. How you might speak with your Warrior, Rebel, or Sexual Self will be different than how you might speak with your Heart.

For dialogues focused on understanding, have your Conductor exercise her or his restraint from *fixing* anything. Understanding is a process that is free from the expectation of fixing a problem right away. There will be other opportunities for solving problems when the time is right, but very often there will simply be a need for understanding, apart from fixing. Refer back to chapter 22 to refresh your memory on how to practice seeking, expressing, and exchanging understandings with others. Practice these skills with any or all of your subpersonalities. If you feel safe in doing so, you can even practice this with some of your shadow characters.

Comforting

Dialogues for the sake of comforting include the skills of expressing and understanding described above. Releasing emotions and having them empathically understood is naturally comforting. This comfort can be further enhanced by various forms of reassurance. Messages of reassurance might include, "This is an important concern that I would like to help you with, and if necessary, I will find help for you from someone we can trust." When concerns have no readily available remedy, another reassuring message is, "I know this is really hard, but I want to assure you that I love you and will stay with you through it no matter what."

As you engage in dialogues with subpersonalities that are distressed, know that your Conductor can provide great comfort just by offering attention, permission to express feelings, understanding, reassurance, compassion, and forgiveness if necessary. Have your Conductor ask questions like, "How can I help you?" or, "Is there anything you're needing?" These are all expressions of love, and love is the greatest source of comfort there is.

Balancing

Balancing refers to the process of regulating the behaviors that are either excessive or deficient. Perhaps you have habits that are out of balance (eating, studying, spending, arguing, being lazy, overindulging with alcohol or drugs, gaming, or pornography). These are examples of behavioral imbalances that may require better regulation. Ordinarily it's the Judge that assumes sole responsibility for controlling behavioral concerns, but when that is done in imbalanced ways, the results can be disappointing and costly. Under circumstances like these, your more balanced Conductor is essential for bringing about better results.

To practice this type of dialogue, start by identifying a behavioral habit that you'd like to modify. Next, identify the subpersonality most likely to be associated with that habit. If you're not clear about which subpersonality you need to address, don't worry. A variation you can use is to identify a "specialist" subpersonality that can be labeled for any particular issue. For instance, you might decide to speak with your inner Eater, Student, Spender, Drinker/Drugger,

Gamer, or Porn Watcher. Have that subpersonality pick a colored marker with your non-dominant hand, and your Conductor choose one with your other hand.

For these dialogues, have your Conductor let the subpersonality know that s/he would like to discuss a concern (rather than complaint). Refer back to the techniques for having peace talks described in chapter 22 for guidance. Make sure your Conductor suspends judgment, seeks a mutual understanding of contrasting values and concerns, invites the subpersonality into a collaborative relationship, negotiates new expectations and agreements, and offers reinforcement with expressions of praise and gratitude. Changing behavioral habits can be a difficult and slow process that requires repeated dialogues over time. However, the most effective changes occur when the *non*-rational/subconscious mind is brought into collaboration with conscious/rational mind. That is what these dialogues are accomplishing.

Behavior modification is a subject that has been studied extensively by research psychologists. There are very specific skills that have proven effective for a wide range of behaviors. Some of your behavioral concerns may be too complicated for you to re-balance without the help of a therapist possessing expertise in the area in which you have concern, so consider seeking that help when necessary. Even still, your dialogues with that part of your psyche will till the soil in preparation for an expert gardening consultant to help you plant and grow new seeds for change.

Managing conflicts

In chapter 12 you were introduced to some of the more common conflicts occurring in the subconscious. That list was not exhaustive, but it may be a good starting point for you to begin practicing your conflict management skills. Take a look back at that chapter to see if there might be a conflict you recognize taking place within your own mind. If you recognize one, have the two subpersonalities involved pick colored markers using either hand. In these dialogues, practice using some of the other skills described in chapter 22. Refer back to the "basic recipe for peace talks" described in that chapter and let your subpersonalities practice those skills with one another.

Conflict management dialogues are often the most challenging to learn to do well. Therefore, start your early dialogues with modest expectations. Don't worry about resolving conflicts right away. Instead, realize that you're learning how to manage conflicts differently. Practice the pursuit of mutual understanding without judgment. Create an intention to foster collaboration between the subpersonalities in conflict. Have them use "I" messages instead of "You" messages, and reflect back to one another what is being heard and understood. Then have them respond with the echoing technique described in that chapter. Allow them to begin negotiating with one another about ways they can arrive at win/win agreements. Give them opportunities for apology and forgiveness if necessary. Have them exchange comments of respect and appreciation for their efforts to reconcile their differences. View these dialogues as a learning experience in which you can observe, experiment, and practice new ways of communicating.

Another recommendation is to regard these practice dialogues as good training for managing conflicts with other people in your life. What's good about learning conflict management in this way is that it's much safer to engage in conflicts with yourself than it may be with others. To do this, use your imagination to have the other person choose a colored marker with your non-dominant hand while your Conductor uses one with your dominant hand. Have your Conductor take the lead using all the skills you've recently learned to manage conflict. Imagine how the other person might respond. This can be a very powerful way to prepare for managing or resolving conflicts with others. It can even be used to resolve conflicts in your mind and heart with people who are no longer in your life.

Healing

Using the skills presented in this book can help you begin healing the wounds from emotional trauma, abuse, conflict, shame, and loss you have experienced in your lifetime. But what does it mean to heal?

Healing can be thought of as the reconnecting of things that have been broken apart. When relationships are broken, they can sometimes be healed through reconciliation. When the Heart is broken, its state of peace is lost, and healing the Heart is the process of bringing it back into the state of peace. Refer back to chapter 8 to refresh your memory of the elements contributing to the healing process.

Painful emotions are what most often cause the divisions and wounds in our psyches. Grief, fear, despair, anger, guilt, and shame are among the most powerful emotions that separate the Heart from peace and create divisions between subpersonalities. Each of these emotions can be soothed by the skills described in this chapter and those in chapters 8 and 22. Often times the most damaging and lasting wounds are those associated with shame. Identifying and healing shame is often more essential for re-creating peace of mind than anything else. Doing so requires great understanding, compassion, release of judgment, forgiveness, and restoration of the isolated part of oneself that was exiled by that shame.

Healing your deeper wounds may require greater expertise from a skilled psychotherapist. Your own dialogues may help prepare you for therapy and assist your therapy once it's underway. Good therapy can be a very healing experience. Great therapy will help you learn how to continue healing yourself.

Summary

This chapter is meant to help you get started practicing new skills for regulating your mind, restoring wholeness, and creating more peace within. It's only a launching pad for you to begin learning the process. No single book can provide a manual for healing all wounds and conflicts. While your destination may be the peace resulting from healing your wounds, life will continue to present you with new ones. Therefore, *the most important destination for you to focus on is the path itself.* Learn to start dialoguing with your inner family and trust the process.

CHAPTER 26

Closing Thoughts and Hopes

It's my hope that reading this book has helped you to understand that it is possible to heal and create more peace in you life, both within your own mind and between yourself and others. The greater hope is that you will cross the threshold from understanding this to the actual experience of these truths by applying them to your mind and your relationships with others.

The biggest challenge of learning any new skill lies with just getting off to a good start. When riding a bicycle, it's a matter of learning to stay balanced on two wheels. When swimming, it's a matter of learning how to stay afloat in water. When healing, it's a matter of transforming conflict into collaboration, and division into wholeness. And, when transforming your mind, it's a matter of learning to access the various parts of your subconscious and create healthier relationships between them. After clearing the initial hurdles of any new skill, the rest becomes a matter of ongoing practice to further improve and automate them. With perseverance and help from skilled others, those challenges will diminish until one day they will become second nature to you. When that happens, you will join the ranks of the peacemakers of the world, possibly even becoming a healer to others. This anxious, angry, and conflicted world we share is always in need of more healers and peacemakers. Those bearing these gifts will possess many great assets benefiting both themselves and others.

At its core, <u>Whole Mind Healing</u> is simply another effort to translate and interpret the Golden Rule. The Golden Rule has been known the world over for thousands of years, but we are continuously challenged to understand it and to learn to live by its masterful wisdom. Following the Golden Rule in life is not nearly as easy or natural as being governed by our survival instincts. And, while it's remarkable that humans all over the world have discovered the wisdom of this code, what we still lack is the universal ability to incorporate its practices into our daily lives. On an evolutionary scale, the Golden Rule might be thought of as a major upgrade for the operating system of the human mind, but one that we have not yet collectively learned how to install and run. Hopefully this book will be an instrument that will help more people learn how to do just that.

The processes of healing, creating peace, and change in general, are all relational in nature. Individuals can do this for themselves by learning to love, control, and modify different parts of themselves through compassionate dialogues. But again, this is not necessarily superior to undergoing these efforts with others who know how to help. As the protagonists in the Wizard of Oz – Dorothy, Scarecrow, Tin Man, and Cowardly Lion – were each in pursuit of missing elements they needed for finding greater wholeness and peace of mind, they benefited from undertaking the journey with one another's help. Banding together on their quest for greater wholeness helped each to discover that what they needed could be found both between and within themselves.

We all eventually need help with our life's journey, and sometimes both the hardest part and the simplest part of getting the help that we need begins with the courage to ask for it. There is help to be found in self-help books and even more from good therapists. Help can come from special family members, friends, teachers, religious leaders, and spiritual guides as well. But it's often easier to find the help that we need if we have a clear understanding of what we're looking for in the first place. These are some of the things I hope that you have gained from reading Whole Mind Healing.

Don't diminish your own sufferings or those of others through comparison. Be respectful and compassionate toward all forms and degrees of suffering, and listen to your wise airline attendants when they tell you to take care of your own needs first before you devote yourself to the needs of others.

If there are bottom lines to take with you from this book, consider these: first, *healing and peace are essentially acts of compassionate love*, and second, *learning to create peace by loving and healing yourself is the place to begin*. It's my hope that you will gain an experience of these truths by practicing them and sharing them with others in your world.

Peace.

APPENDIX A

Important Precautions

The tools and methods being introduced to you in this book are powerful, and, as with all powerful tools, there exists potential for both good and harm. As you consider and explore the exercises in this chapter, emotional safety should always remain your highest priority, even if you are eagerly in need of emotional relief. The subconscious mind holds endless potential for growth, healing, creativity, problem solving, and other wonders. But it is also the repository for intense pain, fear, fury, guilt, shame, and countless emotional scars. *Opening the doors to these territories can be overwhelming and destabilizing for some people, and not being prepared for these possibilities can result in emotional, cognitive, or behavioral instability.* If you have reason to be uncertain of your ability to maintain an adequate level of functional capacity, you are best advised to only consider attempting these exercises with the support of a mental health professional, or not at all.

Accessing the subconscious mind can be a double-edged sword. On the one hand, it's valuable to be in possession of tools capable of reprogramming your mind and improving your life. On the other hand, taking such matters into your own hands can sometimes have adverse consequences. Only you can be the judge of what level of risk to assume for yourself. If you do decide to try these exercises, choose a pace and level of depth that you feel able to process comfortably. Going too far too fast may do more harm than good.

If you are motivated to explore the potential of these exercises but have some hesitation doing so on your own, find a therapist you can feel comfortable with to help you determine if working with this model and with these tools is advisable for you or not. For people with higher degrees of vulnerability associated with their youth, victimization experiences, trauma histories, chemical abuse or dependency issues, suicidal potential, or significant problems with behavioral control, professional assistance is recommended.

Under any circumstances, at any time if you begin to feel overwhelmed, confused, unsafe or out of control, immediately stop these exercises and do not continue unless or until you receive the professional assistance you need.

Loving yourself, healing yourself, taking care of yourself, and being responsible for yourself are all of paramount importance. However, the highest form of self-care is safety.

How and Why Two-Handed Writing Works

The notion and process of two-handed writing is admittedly odd. But it's a process I have used both in my psychotherapy practice with clients and my own personal journaling for over 25 years. I have yet to come across another method as easy or effective as this for the purposes of accessing and processing material in the subconscious. Below is the best explanation I can provide for why and how it works. While this explanation has a foundation in the science of inter-hemispheric brain functioning, I am not aware of any scientific testing or verification of the model. As much as I wish I could get away with saying, "Just try it because it works," people deserve explanations for experiences that are unusual, especially when it comes to something as personal as a method for exploring and changing their minds.

Origins

Two-handed writing is a therapeutic technique that originated in 1973 from the experience of a California-based Art Therapist and educator named Lucia Capacchione, Ph.D. Her discovery of this simple, yet powerful method began in the context of her battle against an auto-immune disorder. As conventional medical interventions continued to fail her, Capacchione slipped into a deep depression, leading her to find a therapist who taught her how to get in touch with the emotions of her "inner child" by writing with her non-dominant hand. This opened doors of expression and released reservoirs of buried pain, as well as joy. As Capacchione began journaling on a more regular basis to process her thoughts and feelings, she one day observed her left hand spontaneously grabbing her pen away from her right hand and answering back to some very critical thoughts running through her mind. This was her first episode of an actual "dialogue" between different sides of her personality using both hands. The effect that it had on her was so profound that she continued the practice, notic-ing ever increasing levels of relief and healing for her mind, body, and emotions. Thus began her lengthy career teaching the method to students, clients, and many others through her numerous books and lectures.

Following is a basic explanation of the of two-handed writing method. More curious readers would be well-served by reading either of Capacchione's original books on the subject (The Power of Your Other Hand, 1988, or Recovery of Your Inner Child, 1991). Reading these books and practicing the exercises in them in the early 1990s greatly assisted my own healing and growth, as well as that of my clients. I have long become accustomed to the initial reactions of raised eyebrows and groans of awkwardness when I first describe this method to my clients (though many take to it without any hesi-tation). Typically within 15 minutes or less, eyebrows are then raised in astonishment. Unusual? Yes. Effective? Remarkably. What I've appreciated most about teaching this method to my clients is that it puts one's growth and healing experience into their own hands, both literally and figuratively. This is a quintessential example of the adage, "Catch a person a fish, feed them for a day. Teach a person to fish, and feed them for a lifetime."

Scientific Underpinnings

It's well-established scientifically that our brains have two hemispheres (right and left) that are specialized for different purposes. The discovery of these specialized purposes dates back to the 1860s from the work of a French physician, Pierre Paul Broca, and subsequently a German physician, anatomist, psychiatrist, and neuropathologist, Karl Wernicke. Different hemispheric functions have since been scientifically examined through state-of-the-art MRI and PET technologies. We now know that the two hemispheres of the brain operate independently from one another to specialize in performing different functions. Popular interpretations of hemispheric differences have held that the left hemisphere is more responsible for language skills and rational/linear thought processes, whereas the right hemisphere is more responsible for the processing of sensation, non-linear (holistic), and creative thinking. In other words, scientists tend to be more left-brained and artists tend to be more right-brained. Unfortunately, these popular interpretations are not entirely accurate, and the truth is more complicated than these popular generalizations suggest.

What is beyond debate are the facts that our two hemispheres operate independently from one another to perform contrasting functions, while at the same time sharing information through the connective brain tissues known as the corpus callosum. The best way to understand their relationship is that *the left and right brain hemispheres are rivals that have the capacity to collaborate with one another*.

A helpful analogy for understanding the relationship between the two hemispheres is the relationship that might exist between two parents. In the "traditional" family structure, the husband might be the breadwinner, disciplinarian, executive manager of finances, and responsible for household repairs and car maintenance. The wife might be the specialist in nurturing the children emotionally and physically, taking charge of domestic responsibilities (shopping, cooking, cleaning and decorating the home), and act as the social director for the family. And while these specialized functions might be completely independent, communication between husband and wife is necessary for the coordination and collaboration of their skills to get all these jobs done better, sometimes independently and sometimes together. However, as times and conditions change, the husband and wife would also be capable of changing roles. The wife could develop all the skills that the husband was previously responsible for, and vice versa. In other words, their skills are neither fixed nor non-transferable. We all know of modern day "non-traditional" family structures where everything gets successfully taken care of regardless of who does what. All of these responsibilities can be managed regardless if there are two males, two females, one of each, or either alone.

The point of the illustration above is that the two hemispheres of the brain are different and can function *both* independently and interdependently, just like different heads of household. There is a tremendous range of "plasticity" in the brain's capabilities, meaning that both hemispheres can adapt to perform new functions, and they can also learn to work together in new ways when trained to do so. The reason that two-handed writing works so well is because it gets the two hemispheres of the brain communicating with one another in ways that maximize their ability to work together instead of working either independently or against one another. Without this type of communication, it would be analogous to a man going to "male training school" and a woman going to "female training school" to each learn their respective functions, and then just putting them together and expecting everything to work out fine. Anyone married for more than a week understands it doesn't work like that. When contrasting parties try to perform their functions in the absence of understanding and cooperation from the other party, the result is friction, chaos, and conflict. In other words, it disturbs the peace of both. The same is true between the two hemispheres of the brain. The two-handed writing technique serves the purpose of activating new communication and collaboration between the two hemispheres of the brain.

APPENDIX C

Biochemistry

If you have invested time and effort in healing and creating greater peace of mind for yourself using the principles and methods in this book and still find yourself suffering, don't lose hope. These methods of cognitive restructuring are not a panacea for all psychological ills. Your state of mind is determined by more than how you think or how you manage conflict. When self-help and professional therapy are not enough for managing the miseries of anxiety, depression, excessive frustration and anger, mood swings, despair, or self-loathing, it may be necessary to consider the influence of your biochemistry on your state of mind.

The brain is a biochemical organ. While changing thinking and behavior patterns does have a significant influence on the brain's biochemistry, causation works in the other direction as well. The biochemistry of the brain exerts strong influences on the mind's patterns of perception, emotion, thinking, and behavior, sometimes in ways that are too powerful to counteract through therapeutic methods alone. When standard therapeutic interventions fail to provide adequate relief for significant symptoms, it may be necessary to seek a medication consultation from your doctor or a psychiatrist. Science and modern medicine are learning more and more about how certain medical conditions have a profound impact on mental health, and it may be important to undergo an evaluation to determine if there are any underlying biological problems negatively affecting the functioning of your mind.

<u>Whole Mind Healing</u> addresses limited parts of what determines an individual's psychology. The principles and techniques offered here can be *useful* for virtually everyone, but that does not mean that they are *adequate* for everyone on their own. The range of other factors influencing mental health goes beyond the scope of this book, but may include genetically inherited mental health disorders, poor diet and nutrition, the impact of environmental toxins on the brain (e.g., viruses, bacteria, heavy metals, pollutants). As much as we have learned about how the brain and mind work and fail to work properly, there is still much that we don't fully comprehend or that has not found its way into the mainstream of our healthcare system.

Physical and mental health are part of the same complex system. Each of these dimensions is able to exert powerful influences on the other. One analogy I frequently use to explain this relationship is that of a radio. Imagine a radio that is tuned into a channel of music or talk that you absolutely hate to listen to, and furthermore that the volume on the radio is turned up to its loudest setting. This would create an extremely unpleasant experience for you. Cognitive restructuring, as prescribed in this book and in many models of psychotherapy, is akin to changing the channel on the radio to one that is more in harmony with your nature, but this may not change the volume. Psychotropic medications and other medical or natural interventions may be the key to turning the volume down on the radio, though such interventions typically have little influence on the channel setting. For many people, finding optimal levels of peace of mind requires making adjustments to both.